THE KUFR OF CHRISTIANS AND JEWS

BY GREGORY HEARY

This book is about the Kufr (Disbelief) of Christians and Jews. It is compiled so nobody is confused whether Muslim or non-Muslim. The evidence for the charges levied is presented from the translated Quran, Tafsir and Hadith with fatwas at the end to summarize the legal verdict proving the charges of disbelief true regardless of who denies or doubts the accuracy of the charges. There are various types of major Kufr (major Disbelief) the Christians and Jews are guilty of in the past, present and will be guilty of in the future as God permits. Some of their categories of Kufr/Disbelief include:

- *Kufr ul-Inkar*: Disbelief out of denial. This applies to someone who denies with both heart and tongue.
- *Kufr ul-Kibr*: Disbelief out of arrogance and pride.
- *Kufr ul-Istihal*: Disbelief out of trying to make forbidden into lawful. This applies to someone who accepts as lawful (*halal*) that which Allah has made unlawful (*haram*) like alcohol, gambling or interest. Only Allah has the authority to make things lawful and forbidden and those who seek to interfere with His right are like rivals to Him and therefore fall outside the boundaries of faith.
- *Kufr ul-Istibdal*: Disbelief because of trying to substitute Allah's Laws. This could take the form of (a) rejection of Allah's Law (*shari'ah*) without denying it, (b) denial of Allah's law and therefore rejecting it, or (c) substituting Allah's laws with man-made laws.

- *Kufr ul-Kurh*: Disbelief out of detesting any of Allah's Commands.
- *Kufr ul-Istihzaha*: Disbelief due to mockery and derision.
- *Kufr ul-I'radh*: Disbelief due to avoidance. This applies to those who turn away and avoid the truth.
- *Kufr ul-Juhud*: Disbelief out of rejection. This applies to someone who acknowledges the truth in his heart, but rejects it with his tongue.
- *Kufr ul-'Inad*: Disbelief out of stubbornness. This applies to someone who knows the truth and admits to knowing the truth and admits to knowing it with his tongue, but refuses to accept it and refrains from making a declaration.

This book refers to Christians and Jews as Christians and Jews instead of Ahl-Kitab, because Ahl-Kitab can also refer to Muslims who used to be Christians or Jews or Zoroastrians. The Jewish and Christian Ahl-Kitab have lost their Kitabs but are still called Ahl-Kitab in Islam because they are descendants of those given Kitabs and a Kitab of Allah is a big thing to have been given, even if one lost it tis still an honor to have once had. Those Ahl-Kitab who become Muslims, are still occasionally called Ahl-Kitab and Allah refers to them as such in the Quran. Yet every Ahl-Kitab Christian or Jew who is not Muslim is a Kafir guilty of the crime of Kufr, and Kufr without repentance (via Islamic Tawbah) leads to eternal Hell.

TEXTUAL EVIDENCE PROVING THE KUFR OF CHRISTIANS AND JEWS

Quran 1:1-7

All the praises and thanks be to Allah, the Lord of the 'Âlamîn (mankind, jinn and all that exists). (2) The Most Gracious, the Most Merciful (3) The Only Owner (and the Only Ruling Judge) of the Day of Recompense (i.e. the Day of Resurrection) (4) You (Alone) we worship, and You (Alone) we ask for help (for each and everything). (5) Guide us to the Straight Way. (6) The Way of those on whom You have bestowed Your Grace, not (the way) of those who earned Your Anger (such as the Jews), nor of those who went astray (such as the Christians).

Narrated 'Adiyy bin Hatim:

that the Prophet said: "The Jews are those who Allah is wrath with, and the Christians have strayed."

Source: Jami at-Tirmidhi

English reference : Vol. 5, Book 44, Hadith 3954

Graded: Hasan by Darussalam

This very first chapter of the Quran, lists 3 categories of Tawheed which Christians all disbelieve in. The very 1st verse is rejected by them because they praise/thank others besides Allah such as prophet Jesus, his mother Mary or their "saintly" figures. Thus the first verse promoting

Tawheed Ibadaah (Oneness of Worship) is a proof that Christians reject and make Shirk of Ibadaah. Christians also reject that Allah is Lord of everything rejecting Tawheed Rububiyyah (Oneness of Lordship/Dominion) by claiming Jesus pbuh is their Lord or that Allah is 3 and the "Holy Spirit" has a claim of divinity and thereby Lordship. The 2nd verse promotes Tawheed Asma wa Sifat (Oneness of Allah's names/attributes) which Christians reject by equating others as more or as merciful as Allah which is why they pray to them rather than Allah hoping their mercifulness motivates them to intercede with Allah making Shirk of Asma wa Sifat. The 3rd verse promotes both Tawheed Asma wa Sifat and Tawheed Rububiyyah (Oneness of Dominion/Lordship) which Christians reject by insisting Jesus pbuh would be Lord on the Day of Judgement thus making Shrik Rububiyyah. Hence in 3 verses Christians reject 3 categories of the exclusive oneness of God, rejecting some types of Tawheed more than once with the fourth verse obviously being rejected by them as they commit shirk in ibadah worshipping others and seeking help from others than Allah. Whereas the final verse of the chapter lists those whom Allah is angered with and have strayed which Prophet Muhammad pbuh explained were the Jews and Christians. Recognizing the popularity of this chapter and the clear Kufr of Christians in its regard and the clarity by the single hadith I've included one would wonder why people would need a book such as this, but many would be surprised by the ignorance of people regarding the basic concept that only two categories of people exist; Muslim and Kafir. However even if such a book were unnecessary it is better to have knowledge you don't need than need knowledge you don't have. Tis a sad era when this book is needed. But even sadder when such knowledge is unknown or even worse denounced. If this book seems unnecessary to you rejoice in the blessing of knowledge. For the rest of the book I will refrain from in-depth analysis of the proofs as they are clearer than sunlight and moonlight despite the metaphorical clouds spread by "reformers", modernists and pluralists who need this book most of all.

Quran 2:6

Verily, those who disbelieve, it is the same to them whether you warn them or do not warn them, they will not believe.

Quran 2:23-24

And if you (Arab pagans, Jews, and Christians) are in doubt concerning that which We have sent down (i.e. the Qur'ân) to Our slave (Muhammad), then produce a Sûrah (chapter) of the like thereof and call your witnesses (supporters and helpers) besides Allâh, if you are truthful. (23) But if you do it not, and you can never do it, then fear the Fire (Hell) whose fuel is men and stones, prepared for the disbelievers.

Quran 2:26

Verily, Allâh is not ashamed to set forth a parable even of a mosquito or so much more when it is bigger (or less when it is smaller) than it. And as for those who believe, they know that it is the Truth from their Lord, but as for those who disbelieve, they say: "What did Allâh intend by this parable?" By it He misleads many, and many He guides thereby. And He misleads thereby only those who are Al-Fâsiqûn (the rebellious, disobedient to Allâh).

Quran 2:40-44

O Children of Israel! Remember My Favour which I bestowed upon you, and fulfill (your obligations to) My Covenant (with you) so that I fulfill (My Obligations to) your covenant (with Me), and fear none but Me. (40) And believe in what I have sent down (this Qur'ân), confirming that which is with you, [the Taurât (Torah) and the Injeel], and be not the first to disbelieve therein, and buy not with My Verses [the Taurât (Torah) and the Injeel] a small price (i.e. getting a small gain by selling My Verses), and fear Me and Me Alone. (41) And mix not truth with falsehood, nor conceal the truth [i.e. Muhammad is Allâh's Messenger and his qualities are written in your Scriptures, the Taurât (Torah) and the Injeel] while you know (the truth) (42)And perform As-Salât (Iqâmat-as-Salât), and give Zakât, and bow down (or submit yourselves with obedience to Allâh) along with Ar¬Raki'ûn. (43) Enjoin you Al-Birr (piety and righteousness and each and every act of obedience to Allâh) on the people and you forget (to practise it) yourselves, while you recite the Scripture [the Taurât (Torah)]! Have you then no sense?

Quran 2:74-101

Then, after that, your hearts were hardened and became as stones or even worse in hardness. And indeed, there are stones out of which rivers gush forth, and indeed, there are of them (stones) which split asunder so that water flows from them, and indeed, there are of them (stones) which fall down for fear of Allâh. And Allâh is not unaware of what you do. (74) Do you (faithful believers) covet that they will believe in your religion inspite of the fact that a party of them (Jewish rabbis) used to hear the Word of Allâh [the Taurât (Torah)], then they used to change it knowingly after they understood it? (75) And when they (Jews) meet those who believe (Muslims), they say, "We believe", but when they meet one another in private, they say, "Shall you (Jews) tell them

(Muslims) what Allâh has revealed to you [Jews, about the description and the qualities of Prophet Muhammad, that which are written in the Taurât (Torah)] , that they (Muslims) may argue with you (Jews) about it before your Lord?" Have you (Jews) then no understanding? (76) Know they (Jews) not that Allâh knows what they conceal and what they reveal? (77) And there are among them (Jews) unlettered people, who know not the Book, but they trust upon false desires and they but guess. (78) Then woe to those who write the Book with their own hands and then say, "This is from Allâh," to purchase with it a little price! Woe to them for what their hands have written and woe to them for that they earn thereby. (79) And they (Jews) say, "The Fire (i.e. Hell-fire on the Day of Resurrection) shall not touch us but for a few numbered days." Say: "Have you taken a covenant from Allâh, so that Allâh will not break His Covenant? Or is it that you say of Allâh what you know not?" (80) Yes! Whosoever earns evil and his sin has surrounded him, they are dwellers of the Fire (i.e. Hell); they will dwell therein forever. (81) And those who believe (in the Oneness of Allâh- Islâmic Monotheism) and do righteous good deeds, they are dwellers of Paradise, they will dwell therein forever. (82) And (remember) when We took a covenant from the Children of Israel, (saying): Worship none but Allâh (Alone) and be dutiful and good to parents, and to kindred, and to orphans and Al-Masâkîn (the poor), and speak good to people [i.e. enjoin righteousness and forbid evil, and say the truth about Muhammad], and perform As-Salât, and give Zakât. Then you slid back, except a few of you, while you are backsliders. (83) And (remember) when We took your covenant (saying): Shed not the blood of your (people), nor turn out your own people from their dwellings. Then, (this) you ratified and (to this) you bear witness. (84) After this, it is you who kill one another and drive out a party of you from their homes, assist (their enemies) against them, in sin and transgression. And if they come to you as captives, you ransom them, although their expulsion was forbidden to you. Then do you believe in a part of the Scripture and reject the rest? Then what is the recompense of those who do so among you, except disgrace in the life of this world, and on the Day of Resurrection they shall be consigned to the most grievous torment. And Allâh is not unaware of what you do. (85) Those are they who have bought the life of this world at the price of the Hereafter. Their torment shall not be lightened nor shall they be helped. (86) And indeed, We gave Mûsa (Moses) the Book and followed him up with a succession of Messengers. And We gave 'Īsā (Jesus), the son of Maryam (Mary), clear signs and supported him with Rûh-ul-Qudus [Jibrael (Gabriel)]. Is it that whenever there came to you a Messenger with what you yourselves desired not, you grew arrogant? Some you disbelieved and some you killed. (87) And they say, "Our hearts are wrapped (i.e. do not hear or understand Allâh's Word)." Nay, Allâh has cursed them for their disbelief, so little is that which they believe. (88) And when there came to them (the Jews), a Book (this Qur'ân) from Allâh confirming what is with them [the Taurât (Torah) and the Injeel], although aforetime they had invoked Allâh (for coming of Muhammad) in order to gain victory over those who disbelieved, then when there came to them that which they had recognized, they disbelieved in it. So let the Curse of Allâh be on the disbelievers. (89) How bad is that for which they have sold their ownselves, that they should disbelieve in that which Allâh has revealed (the Qur'ân), grudging that Allâh should reveal of His Grace unto whom He wills of His slaves. So they have drawn on themselves wrath upon wrath. And for the disbelievers, there is disgracing torment. (90) And when it is said to them, "Believe in what Allâh has sent down," they say, "We believe in what was sent down to us." And they disbelieve in that which came after it, while it is the truth confirming what is with them. Say: "Why then have you *killed the Prophets of Allâh aforetime, if you indeed have been believers?" (91) And indeed Mûsa (Moses) came to you with clear proofs, yet you worshipped the calf after he left, and you were Zâlimûn (polytheists and wrong-doers). (92) And (remember) when We took your covenant and We raised above you the Mount (saying), "Hold firmly to what We have given you and hear (Our Word). They said, "We have heard and disobeyed." And their hearts absorbed (the worship of) the calf because of their disbelief. Say: "Worst indeed is that which your faith enjoins on you if you are believers." (93) Say to (them): "If the home of the Hereafter with Allâh is indeed for you specially and not for others, of mankind, then long for death if you are truthful." (94) But they will never long for it because of what their hands have sent before them (i.e. what they have done). And Allâh is All-Aware of the Zâlimûn (polytheists and wrong-doers) (95) And verily, you will find them (the Jews) the greediest of mankind for life and (even greedier) than those who ascribe partners to Allâh (and do not believe in Resurrection - Majus, pagans, and idolaters). Everyone of them wishes that he could be given a life of a thousand years. But the grant of such life will not save him even a little from (due) punishment. And Allâh is All-Seer of what they do. (96)Say (O Muhammad): "Whoever is an enemy to Jibrael (Gabriel) (let him die in his fury), for indeed he has brought it (this Qur'ân) down to your heart by Allâh's Permission, confirming what came before it [i.e. the Taurât (Torah) and the Injeel] and guidance and glad tidings for the believers. (97) "Whoever is an enemy to Allâh, His Angels, His Messengers, Jibrael (Gabriel) and Mikael (Michael), then verily, Allâh is an enemy to the disbelievers." (98) And indeed We have sent down to you manifest Ayât (these Verses of the Qur'ân which inform in detail about the news of the Jews and their secret intentions, etc.), and none disbelieve in them but Fâsiqûn (those who rebel against Allâh's Command). (99) Is it not (the case) that every time they make a covenant, some party among them throw it aside? Nay! (the truth) is most of them believe not. (100) And when there came to them a Messenger from Allâh (i.e. Muhammad) confirming what was with them, a party of those who were given the Scripture threw away the Book of Allâh behind their backs as if they did not know!*

Quran 2:105

Neither those who disbelieve among the people of the Scripture (Jews and Christians) nor Al-Mushrikûn (the idolaters, polytheists, disbelievers in the Oneness of Allâh, pagans, etc.) like that there should be sent down unto you any good from your Lord. But Allâh chooses for His Mercy whom He wills. And Allâh is the Owner of Great Bounty.

Quran 2:109

Many of the people of the Scripture (Jews and Christians) wish that if they could turn you away as disbelievers after you have believed, out of envy from their ownselves, even after the truth (that Muhammad Peace be upon him is Allâh's Messenger) has become manifest unto them. But forgive and overlook, till Allâh brings His Command. Verily, Allâh is Able to do all things.

Quran 2:111-121

And they say, "None shall enter Paradise unless he be a Jew or a Christian." These are their own desires. Say, "Produce your proof if you are truthful." (111) Yes, but whoever submits his face (himself) to Allâh (i.e. follows Allâh's Religion of Islâmic Monotheism) and he is a Muhsin then his reward is with his Lord (Allâh), on such shall be no fear, nor shall they grieve. (112) The Jews said that the Christians follow nothing (i.e. are not on the right religion); and the Christians said that the Jews follow nothing (i.e. are not on the right religion); though they both recite the Scripture. Like unto their word, said (the pagans) who know not. Allâh will judge between them on the Day of Resurrection about that wherein they have been differing. (113) And who are more unjust than those who forbid that Allâh's Name be glorified and mentioned much (i.e. prayers and invocations, etc.) in Allâh's mosques and strive for their ruin? It was not fitting that such should themselves enter them (Allâh's Mosques) except in fear. For them there is disgrace in this world, and they will have a great torment in the Hereafter. (114) And to Allâh belong the east and the west, so wherever you turn (yourselves or your faces) there is the Face of Allâh (and He is High above, over His Throne). Surely! Allâh is All-Sufficient for His creatures' needs, All-Knowing. (115) And they (Jews, Christians and pagans) say: Allâh has begotten a son (children or offspring). Glory be to Him (Exalted be He above all that they associate with Him). Nay, to Him belongs all that is in the heavens and on earth, and all surrender with obedience (in worship) to Him. (116) The Originator of the heavens and the earth. When He decrees a matter, He only says to it : "Be!" - and it is. (117) And those who have no knowledge say: "Why does not Allâh speak to us (face to face) or why does not a sign come to us?" So said the people before them words of similar import. Their hearts are alike, We have indeed made plain the signs for people who believe with certainty. (118) Verily, We have sent you (O Muhammad) with the truth (Islâm), a bringer of glad tidings (for those who believe in what you brought, that they will enter Paradise) and a warner (for those who disbelieve in what you brought, they will enter the Hell-fire). And you will not be asked about the dwellers of the blazing Fire. (119) Never will the Jews nor the Christians be pleased with you till you follow their religion. Say: "Verily, the Guidance of Allâh (i.e. Islâmic Monotheism) that is the (only) Guidance. And if you were to *follow their (Jews and Christians) desires after what you have received of Knowledge (i.e. the Qur'ân), then you would have against Allâh neither any Walî (protector or guardian) nor any helper. (120) Those (who embraced Islâm from Banî Israel) to whom We gave the Book [the Taurât (Torah)] [or those (Muhammad's Peace be upon him companions) to whom We have given the Book (the Qur'ân)] recite it (i.e. obey its orders and follow its teachings) as it should be recited (i.e. followed), they are the ones that believe therein. And whoso disbelieves in it (the Qur'ân), those are they who are the losers.*

Quran 2:135-140

And they say, "Be Jews or Christians, then you will be guided." Say "Nay, (We follow) only the religion of Ibrâhim (Abraham), Hanifa [Islâmic Monotheism, i.e. to worship none but Allâh (Alone)], and he was not of Al-Mushrikûn (those who worshipped others along with Allâh)." (135) Say (O Muslims), "We believe in Allâh and that which has been sent down to us and that which has been sent down to Ibrâhim (Abraham), Ismâ'il (Ishmael), Ishâq (Isaac), Ya'qûb (Jacob), and to Al-Asbât [the offspring twelve sons of Ya'qûb (Jacob)], and that which has been given to Mûsa (Moses) and Isâ (Jesus), and that which has been given to the Prophets from their Lord. We make no distinction between any of them, and to Him we have submitted (in Islâm)." (136) So if they believe in the like of that which you believe, then they are rightly guided, but if they turn away, then they are only in opposition. So Allâh will suffice for you against them. And He is the All-Hearer, the All-Knower. (137) [Our Sibghah (religion) is] the Sibghah (Religion) of Allâh (Islâm) and which Sibghah (religion) can be better than Allâh's? And we are His worshippers. (138) Say "Dispute you with us about Allâh while He is our Lord and your Lord? And we are to be rewarded for our deeds and you for your deeds. And we are sincere to Him [in worship and obedience (i.e. we worship Him Alone and none else, and we obey His Orders).]" (139) Or say you that Ibrâhim (Abraham), Ismâ'il (Ishmael), Ishâque (Isaac), Ya'qûb (Jacob) and Al-Asbât [the offspring twelve sons of Ya'qûb (Jacob)] were Jews or Christians? Say, "Do you know better or does Allâh (know better... that they all were Muslims)? And who is more unjust than he who conceals the testimony [i.e. to believe in Prophet Muhammad when he comes, as is written in their Books.] he has from Allâh? And Allâh is not unaware of what you do."

Quran 2:145-147

And even if you were to bring to the people of the Scripture (Jews and Christians) all the Ayât (proofs, evidences, verses, lessons, signs, revelations, etc.), they would not follow your Qiblah (prayer direction), nor are you going to follow their Qiblah (prayer direction). And they will not follow each other's Qiblah (prayer direction). Verily, if you follow their desires after that which you have received of knowledge (from Allâh), then indeed you will be one of the Zâlimûn (polytheists, wrong-doers.) (145) Those to whom We gave the Scripture (Jews and Christians) recognize him (Muhammad) as they recognize their sons. But verily, a party of them conceal the truth while they know it - [i.e. the qualities of Muhammad which are written in the Taurât (Torah) and the Injeel]. (146) (This is) the truth from your Lord. So be you not one of those who doubt.

Quran 2:159-162

Verily, those who conceal the clear proofs, evidences and the guidance, which We have sent down, after We have made it clear for the people in the Book, they are the ones cursed by Allâh and cursed by the cursers. (159) Except those who repent and do righteous deeds, and openly declare (the truth which they concealed). These, I will accept their repentance. And I am the One Who accepts repentance, the Most Merciful. (160) Verily, those who disbelieve, and die while they are disbelievers, it is they on whom is the Curse of Allâh and of the angels and of mankind, combined. (161) They will abide therein (under the curse in Hell), their punishment will neither be lightened, nor will they be reprieved.

Quran 2:165-171

And of mankind are some who take (for worship) others besides Allâh as rivals (to Allâh). They love them as they love Allâh. But those who believe, love Allâh more (than anything else). If only, those who do wrong could see, when they will see the torment, that all power belongs to Allâh and that Allâh is Severe in punishment. (165) When those who were followed, disown (declare themselves innocent of) those who followed (them), and they see the torment, then all their relations will be cut off from them. (166) And those who followed will say: "If only we had one more chance to return (to the worldly life), we would disown (declare ourselves as innocent from) them as they have disowned (declared themselves as innocent from) us." Thus Allâh will show them their deeds as regrets for them. And they will never get out of the Fire. (167) O mankind! Eat of that which is lawful and good on the earth, and follow not the footsteps of Shaitân (Satan). Verily, he is to you an open enemy: (168) He [Shaitân (Satan)] commands you only what is evil and Fahshâ (sinful), and that you should say against Allâh what you know not. (169) When it is said to them: "Follow what Allâh has sent down." They say: "Nay! We shall follow what we found our fathers following." (Would they do that!) even though their fathers did not understand anything nor were they guided? (170) And the example of those who disbelieve, is as that of him who shouts to those (flock of sheep) that hears nothing but calls and cries. (They are) deaf, dumb and blind. So they do not understand.

Quran 2:174-176

Verily, those who conceal what Allâh has sent down of the Book, and purchase a small gain therewith (of worldly things), they eat into their bellies nothing but fire. Allâh will not speak to them on the Day of Resurrection, nor purify them, and theirs will be a painful torment. (174) Those are they who have purchased error at the price of Guidance, and torment at the price of Forgiveness. So how bold they are (for evil deeds which will push them) to the Fire. (175) That is because Allâh has sent down the Book (the Qur'ân) in truth. And verily, those who disputed as regards the Book are far away in opposition.

Quran 2:211-213

Ask the Children of Israel how many clear Ayât (proofs, evidences, verses, lessons, signs, revelations, etc.) We gave them. And whoever changes Allâh's Favour after it had come to him, [e.g. renounces the Religion of Allâh (Islâm) and accepts Kufr (disbelief),] then surely, Allâh is Severe in punishment. (211) Beautified is the life of this world for those who disbelieve, and they mock at those who believe. But those who obey Allâh's Orders and keep away from what He has forbidden, will be above them on the Day of Resurrection. And Allâh gives (of His Bounty, Blessings, Favours, Honours, on the Day of Resurrection) to whom He wills without limit. (212) Mankind were one community and Allâh sent Prophets with glad tidings and warnings, and with them He sent the Scripture in truth to judge between people in matters wherein they differed. And only those to whom (the Scripture) was given differed concerning it after clear proofs had come unto them through hatred, one to another. Then Allâh by His Leave guided those who believed to the truth of that wherein they differed. And Allâh guides whom He wills to a Straight Path.

Quran 2:252-253

These are the Verses of Allâh, We recite them to you (O Muhammad) in truth, and surely, you are one of the Messengers (of Allâh). (252) Those Messengers! We preferred some often to others; to some of them Allâh spoke (directly); others He raised to degrees (of honour); and to 'Îsâ (Jesus), the son of Maryam (Mary), We gave clear proofs and evidences, and supported him with Rûh-ul-Qudus [Jibrael (Gabriel)]. If Allâh had willed, succeeding generations would not have fought against each other, after clear Verses of Allâh had come to them, but they differed - some of them believed and others disbelieved. If Allâh had willed, they would not have fought against one another, but Allâh does what He likes.

Quran 2:256-257

There is no compulsion in religion. Verily, the Right Path has become distinct from the wrong path. Whoever disbelieves in Tâghût and believes in Allâh, then he has grasped the most trustworthy handhold that will never break. And Allâh is All-Hearer, All-Knower. (256) Allâh is the Walî (Protector or Guardian) of those who believe. He brings them out from darkness into light. But as for those who disbelieve, their Auliyâ (supporters and helpers) are Tâghût [false deities and false leaders], they bring them out from light into darkness. Those are the dwellers of the Fire, and they will abide therein forever.

It was reported that the Ansar were the reason behind revealing these Ayah, although its indication is general in meaning. Ibn Jarir recorded that Ibn `Abbas said that before Islam, "When (an Ansar) woman would not bear children who would live, she would vow that if she gives birth to a child who remains alive, she would raise him as a Jew. When Banu An-Nadir (the Jewish tribe) were evacuated from Al-Madinah, some of the children of the Ansar were being raised among them, and the Ansar said, `We will not abandon our children.' Allah revealed,

"There is no compulsion in religion. Verily, the right path has become distinct from the wrong path.''

Abu Dawud and An-Nasa'i also recorded this Hadith.

Quran 3:2-4

Allâh! Lâ ilahâ illa Huwa (none has the right to be worshipped but He), the Ever Living, the One Who sustains and protects all that exists. (2) It is He Who has sent down the Book (the Qur'ân) to you (Muhammad) with truth, confirming what came before it. And he sent down the Taurât (Torah) and the Injeel (3)Aforetime, as a guidance to mankind, And He sent down the criterion [of judgement between right and wrong (this Qur'ân)]. Truly, those who disbelieve in the Ayât (proofs, evidences, verses, lessons, signs, revelations, etc.) of Allâh, for them there is a severe torment; and Allâh is All-Mighty, All-Able of Retribution.

Quran 3:19-25

Truly, the religion with Allâh is Islâm. Those who were given the Scripture (Jews and Christians) did not differ except, out of mutual jealousy, after knowledge had come to them. And whoever disbelieves in the Ayât (proofs, evidences, verses, signs, revelations, etc.) of Allâh, then surely, Allâh is Swift in calling to account. (19) So if they dispute with you (Muhammad) say: "I have submitted myself to Allâh (in Islâm), and (so have) those who follow me." And say to those who were given the Scripture (Jews

and Christians) and to those who are illiterates (Arab pagans):
"Do you (also) submit yourselves (to Allâh in Islâm)?" If they do,
they are rightly guided; but if they turn away, your duty is only to
convey the Message; and Allâh is All-Seer of (His) slaves (20)
Verily! Those who disbelieve in the Ayât (proofs, evidences, verses,
lessons, signs, revelations, etc.) of Allâh and kill the Prophets
without right, and kill those men who order just dealings, ... then
announce to them a painful torment. (21) They are those whose
works will be lost in this world and in the Hereafter, and they will
have no helpers. (22) Have you not seen those who have been given
a portion of the Scripture? They are being invited to the Book of
Allâh to settle their dispute, then a party of them turn away, and
they are averse. (23) This is because they say: "The Fire shall not
touch us but for a number of days." And that which they used to
invent regarding their religion has deceived them. (24) How (will
it be) when We gather them together on the Day about which there
is no doubt (i.e. the Day of Resurrection). And each person will be
paid in full what he has earned? And they will not be dealt with
unjustly.

Quran 3:31-32

Say (O Muhammad to mankind): "If you (really) love Allâh then
follow me (i.e. accept Islâmic Monotheism, follow the Qur'ân and
the Sunnah), Allâh will love you and forgive you your sins. And
Allâh is Oft-Forgiving, Most Merciful." (31) Say: "Obey Allâh
and the Messenger (Muhammad)." But if they turn away, then
Allâh does not like the disbelievers

Quran 3:52-91

Then when 'Īsā (Jesus) came to know of their disbelief, he said:
"Who will be my helpers in Allâh's Cause?" Al-Hawâriyyûn (the
disciples) said: "We are the helpers of Allâh; we believe in Allâh,

and bear witness that we are Muslims (i.e. we submit to Allâh)."
(52) Our Lord! We believe in what You have sent down, and we
follow the Messenger ['Isâ (Jesus)]; so write us down among those
who bear witness (to the truth i.e. Lâ ilâha ill-Allâh - none has the
right to be worshipped but Allâh) (53) And they (disbelievers)
plotted [to kill 'Isâ (Jesus)], and Allâh plotted too. And Allâh is the
Best of those who plot. (54) And (remember) when Allâh said: "O
'Isâ (Jesus)! I will take you and raise you to Myself and clear you
[of the forged statement that 'Isâ (Jesus) is Allâh's son] of those
who disbelieve, and I will make those who follow you (Monotheists,
who worship none but Allâh) superior to those who disbelieve [in
the Oneness of Allâh, or disbelieve in some of His Messengers, e.g.
Muhammad, 'Isâ (Jesus), Mûsâ (Moses), etc., or in His Books, e.g.
the Taurât (Torah), the Injeel, the Qur'ân] till the Day of
Resurrection. Then you will return to Me and I will judge between
you in the matters in which you used to dispute." (55) "As to
those who disbelieve, I will punish them with a severe torment in
this world and in the Hereafter, and they will have no helpers."
(56) And as for those who believe (in the Oneness of Allâh) and do
righteous good deeds, Allâh will pay them their reward in full.
And Allâh does not like the Zâlimûn (polytheists and wrong-
doers). (57) This is what We recite to you (O Muhammad) of the
Verses and the Wise Reminder (i.e. the Qur'ân) (58) Verily, the
likeness of 'Isâ (Jesus) before Allâh is the likeness of Adam. He
created him from dust, then (He) said to him: "Be!" - and he was.
(59) (This is) the truth from your Lord, so be not of those who
doubt. (60) Then whoever disputes with you concerning him ['Isâ
(Jesus)] after (all this) knowledge that has come to you, [i.e. 'Isâ
(Jesus)] being a slave of Allâh, and having no share in Divinity)
say: "Come, let us call our sons and your sons, our women and
your women, ourselves and yourselves - then we pray and invoke
(sincerely) the Curse of Allâh upon those who lie." (61) Verily!

This is the true narrative [about the story of 'Īsā (Jesus)], and, Lâ ilâha ill-Allâh (none has the right to be worshipped but Allâh, the One and the Only True God, Who has neither a wife nor a son). And indeed, Allâh is the All-Mighty, the All-Wise. (62) And if they turn away (and do not accept these true proofs and evidences), then surely, Allâh is All-Aware of those who do mischief. (63) Say: "O people of the Scripture (Jews and Christians): Come to a word that is just between us and you, that we worship none but Allâh (Alone), and that we associate no partners with Him, and that none of us shall take others as lords besides Allâh. Then, if they turn away, say: "Bear witness that we are Muslims." (64) O people of the Scripture (Jews and Christians)! Why do you dispute about Ibrâhim (Abraham), while the Taurât (Torah) and the Injeel were not revealed till after him? Have you then no sense? (65) Verily, you are those who have disputed about that of which you have knowledge. Why do you then dispute concerning that of which you have no knowledge? It is Allâh Who knows, and you know not. (66) Ibrâhim (Abraham) was neither a Jew nor a Christian, but he was a true Muslim Hanifa (Islâmic Monotheism - to worship none but Allâh Alone) and he was not of Al-Mushrikûn (67) Verily, among mankind who have the best claim to Ibrâhim (Abraham) are those who followed him, and this Prophet (Muhammad) and those who have believed (Muslims). And Allâh is the Walî (Protector and Helper) of the believers. (68) A party of the people of the Scripture (Jews and Christians) wish to lead you astray. But they shall not lead astray anyone except themselves, and they perceive not. (69) O people of the Scripture! (Jews and Christians): "Why do you disbelieve in the Ayât of Allâh, [the Verses about Prophet Muhammad present in the Taurât (Torah) and the Injeel] while you (yourselves) bear witness (to their truth)." (70) O people of the Scripture (Jews and Christians): "Why do you mix truth with falsehood and conceal *the truth while you know?" (71) And a party of the people of the Scripture say: "Believe in the morning in that which is revealed to the believers (Muslims), and reject it at the end of the day, so that they may turn back. (72) And believe no one except the one who follows your religion. Say (O Muhammad): "Verily! Right guidance is the Guidance of Allâh" and do not believe that anyone can receive like that which you have received (of Revelation) except when he follows your religion, otherwise they would engage you in argument before your Lord. Say (O Muhammad): "All the bounty is in the Hand of Allâh; He grants to whom He wills. And Allâh is All-Sufficient for His creatures' needs, the All-Knower." (73) He selects for His Mercy (Islâm and the Qur'ân with Prophethood) whom He wills and Allâh is the Owner of Great Bounty. (74) Among the people of the Scripture (Jews and Christians) is he who, if entrusted with a Qintar (a great amount of wealth, etc.), will readily pay it back; and among them there is he who, if entrusted with a single silver coin, will not repay it unless you constantly stand demanding, because they say: "There is no blame on us to betray and take the properties of the illiterates (Arabs)." But they tell a lie against Allâh while they know it. (75) Yes, whoever fulfils his pledge and fears Allâh much; verily, then Allâh loves those who are Al-Muttaqûn (the pious). (76) Verily, those who purchase a small gain at the cost of Allâh's Covenant and their oaths, they shall have no portion in the Hereafter (Paradise). Neither will Allâh speak to them, nor look at them on the Day of Resurrection, nor will He purify them, and they shall have a painful torment. (77) And verily, among them is a party who distort the Book with their tongues (as they read), so that you may think it is from the Book, but it is not from the Book, and they say: "This is from Allâh," but it is not from Allâh; and they speak a lie against Allâh while they know it. (78) It is not (possible) for any human being to whom Allâh has given the Book and Al-Hukm (the knowledge and understanding of the laws of religion) and Prophethood to say to the people: "Be my worshippers rather than Allâh's." On the contrary (he would say): "Be you Rabbaniyyun (learned men of religion who practise what they know and also preach others), because you are teaching the Book, and you are studying it." (79) Nor would he order you to take angels and Prophets for lords (gods). Would he order you to disbelieve after you have submitted to Allâh's Will? (80) And (remember) when Allâh took the Covenant of the Prophets, saying: "Take whatever I gave you from the Book and Hikmah (understanding of the Laws of Allâh), and afterwards there will come to you a Messenger (Muhammad) confirming what is with you; you must, then, believe in him and help him." Allâh said: "Do you agree (to it) and will you take up My Covenant (which I conclude with you)?" They said: "We agree." He said: "Then bear witness; and I am with you among the witnesses (for this)." (81) Then whoever turns away after this, they are the Fâsiqûn (rebellious: those who turn away from Allâh's Obedience). (82) Do they seek other than the religion of Allâh (the true Islâmic Monotheism worshipping none but Allâh Alone), while to Him submitted all creatures in the heavens and the earth, willingly or unwillingly. And to Him shall they all be returned. (83) Say: "We believe in Allâh and in what has been sent down to us, and what was sent down to Ibrâhim (Abraham), Ismâ'il (Ishmael), Ishâq (Isaac), Ya'qûb (Jacob) and Al-Asbât [the offspring twelve sons of Ya'qûb (Jacob)] and what was given to Mûsa (Moses), 'Īsā (Jesus) and the Prophets from their Lord. We make no distinction between one another among them and to Him (Allâh) we have submitted (in Islâm)." (84) And whoever seeks a religion other than Islâm, it will never be accepted of him, and in the Hereafter he will be one of the losers. (85) How shall Allâh guide a people who disbelieved after their belief and after they bore witness that the Messenger (Muhammad) is true and after clear*

*proofs had come unto them? And Allâh guides not the people who
are Zâlimûn (polytheists and wrong-doers). (86) They are those
whose recompense is that on them (rests) the Curse of Allâh, of the
angels, and of all mankind. (87) They will abide therein (Hell).
Neither will their torment be lightened, nor will it be delayed or
postponed (for a while). (88) Except for those who repent after that
and do righteous deeds. Verily, Allâh is Oft-Forgiving, Most
Merciful. (89) Verily, those who disbelieved after their Belief and
then went on increasing in their disbelief (i.e. disbelief in the
Qur'ân and in Prophet Muhammad) - never will their repentance
be accepted [because they repent only by their tongues and not
from their hearts]. And they are those who are astray. (90) Verily,
those who disbelieved, and died while they were disbelievers, the
(whole) earth full of gold will not be accepted from anyone of them
even if they offered it as a ransom. For them is a painful torment
and they will have no helpers.*

Quran 3:98-100

*Say: "O people of the Scripture (Jews and Christians)! Why do you
reject the Ayât of Allâh (proofs, evidences, verses, lessons, signs,
revelations, etc.) while Allâh is Witness to what you do?" (98)
Say: "O people of the Scripture (Jews and Christians)! Why do you
stop those who have believed, from the Path of Allâh, seeking to
make it seem crooked, while you (yourselves) are witnesses [to
Muhammad as a Messenger of Allâh and Islâm (Allâh's Religion,
i.e. to worship none but Him Alone)]? And Allâh is not unaware
of what you do." (99) O you who believe! If you obey a group of
those who were given the Scripture (Jews and Christians), they
would (indeed) render you disbelievers after you have believed!*

Quran 3:110-120

You [true believers in Islâmic Monotheism, and real followers of Prophet Muhammad and his Sunnah] are the best of peoples ever raised up for mankind; you enjoin Al-Ma'rûf (i.e. Islâmic Monotheism and all that Islâm has ordained) and forbid Al-Munkar (polytheism, disbelief and all that Islâm has forbidden), and you believe in Allâh. And had the people of the Scripture (Jews and Christians) believed, it would have been better for them; among them are some who have faith, but most of them are Al-Fâsiqûn (disobedient to Allâh - and rebellious against Allâh's Command). (110) They will do you no harm, barring a trifling annoyance; and if they fight against you, they will show you their backs, and they will not be helped. (111) Indignity is put over them wherever they may be, except when under a covenant (of protection) from Allâh, and from men; they have drawn on themselves the Wrath of Allâh, and destruction is put over them. This is because they disbelieved in the Ayât (proofs, evidences, verses, lessons, signs, revelations, etc.) of Allâh and killed the Prophets without right. This is because they disobeyed (Allâh) and used to transgress beyond bounds (in Allâh's disobedience, crimes and sins). (112) Not all of them are alike; a party of the people of the Scripture stand for the right, they recite the Verses of Allâh during the hours of the night, prostrating themselves in prayer. (113) They believe in Allâh and the Last Day; they enjoin Al-Ma'rûf (Islâmic Monotheism, and following Prophet Muhammad) and forbid Al-Munkar (polytheism, disbelief and opposing Prophet Muhammad); and they hasten in (all) good works; and they are among the righteous. (114) And whatever good they do, nothing will be rejected of them; for Allâh knows well those who are Al-Muttaqûn (the pious). (115) Surely, those who reject Faith (disbelieve Allah and in Muhammad as being Allâh's Messenger and in all that which he has brought from Allâh), neither their properties, nor their offspring will avail them aught against Allâh.

They are the dwellers of the Fire, therein they will abide. (116) The likeness of what they spend in this world is the likeness of a wind which is extremely cold; it struck the harvest of a people who did wrong against themselves and destroyed it, (i.e. the good deed of a person is only accepted if he is a monotheist and believes in all the Prophets of Allâh, including Jesus and Muhammad). Allâh wronged them not, but they wronged themselves. (117) O you who believe! Take not as (your) Bitânah (advisors, consultants, protectors, helpers, friends) those outside your religion (pagans, Jews, Christians, and hypocrites) since they will not fail to do their best to corrupt you. They desire to harm you severely. Hatred has already appeared from their mouths, but what their breasts conceal is far worse. Indeed We have made plain to you the Ayât (proofs, evidences, verses) if you understand. (118) Lo! You are the ones who love them but they love you not, and you believe in all the Scriptures [i.e. you believe in the Taurât (Torah) and the Injeel, while they disbelieve in your Book, the Qur'ân]. And when they meet you, they say, "We believe". But when they are alone, they bite the tips of their fingers at you in rage. Say: "Perish in your rage. Certainly, Allâh knows what is in the breasts (all the secrets)." (119) If a good befalls you, it grieves them, but if some evil overtakes you, they rejoice at it. But if you remain patient and become Al-Muttaqûn (the pious), not the least harm will their cunning do to you. Surely, Allâh surrounds all that they do.

Quran 3:181-188

Indeed, Allâh has heard the statement of those (Jews) who say: "Truly, Allâh is poor and we are rich!" We shall record what they have said and their killing of the Prophets unjustly, and We shall say: "Taste you the torment of the burning (Fire)." (181) This is because of that (evil) which your hands have sent before you. And certainly, Allâh is never unjust to (His) slaves. (182) Those (Jews) who said: "Verily, Allâh has taken our promise not to believe in any Messenger unless he brings to us an offering which the fire (from heaven) shall devour." Say: "Verily, there came to you Messengers before me, with clear signs and even with what you speak of; why then did you kill them, if you are truthful?" (183) Then if they reject you (O Muhammad), so were Messengers rejected before you, who came with Al-Baiyyinât (clear signs, proofs, evidences) and the Scripture and the Book of Enlightenment. (184) Everyone shall taste death. And only on the Day of Resurrection shall you be paid your wages in full. And whoever is removed away from the Fire and admitted to Paradise, he indeed is successful. The life of this world is only the enjoyment of deception (a deceiving thing). (185) You shall certainly be tried and tested in your wealth and properties and in your personal selves, and you shall certainly hear much that will grieve you from those who received the Scripture before you (Jews and Christians) and from those who ascribe partners to Allâh; but if you persevere patiently, and become Al-Muttaqûn (the pious) then verily, that will be a determining factor in all affairs (and that is from the great matters which you must hold on with all your efforts). (186) (And remember) when Allâh took a covenant from those who were given the Scripture (Jews and Christians) to make it (the news of the coming of Prophet Muhammad and the religious knowledge) known and clear to mankind, and not to hide it, but they threw it away behind their backs, and purchased with it some miserable gain! And indeed worst is that which they bought. (187) Think not that those who rejoice in what they have done (or brought about), and love to be praised for what they have not done,- think not you that they are rescued from the torment, and for them is a painful torment.

Quran 4:44-57

Have you not seen those who were given a portion of the book, purchasing the wrong path, and wish that you should go astray from the Right Path. (44) Allâh has full knowledge of your enemies, and Allâh is Sufficient as a Walî (Protector), and Allâh is Sufficient as a Helper. (45) Among those who are Jews, there are some who displace words from (their) right places and say: "We hear your word (O Muhammad) and disobey," and "Hear and let you (O Muhammad) hear nothing." And Râ'ina with a twist of their tongues and as a mockery of the religion (Islâm). And if only they had said: "We hear and obey", and "Do make us understand," it would have been better for them, and more proper, but Allâh has cursed them for their disbelief, so they believe not except a few. (46) O you who have been given the Scripture (Jews and Christians)! Believe in what We have revealed (to Muhammad) confirming what is (already) with you, before We efface faces (by making them like the back of necks; without nose, mouth, eyes) and turn them hindwards, or curse them as We cursed the Sabbath¬breakers. And the Commandment of Allâh is always executed. (47) Verily, Allâh forgives not that partners should be set up with Him (in worship), but He forgives except that (anything else) to whom He wills; and whoever sets up partners with Allâh in worship, he has indeed invented a tremendous sin. (48) Have you not seen those (Jews and Christians) who claim sanctity for themselves. Nay, but Allâh sanctifies whom He wills, and they will not be dealt with injustice even equal to the extent of a scalish thread in the long slit of a date-stone. (49) Look, how they invent a lie against Allâh, and enough is that as a manifest sin. (50) Have you not seen those who were given a portion of the Scripture? They believe in Jibt and Tâghût and say to the disbelievers that they are better guided as regards the way than the believers (Muslims). (51) They are those whom Allâh has cursed, and he whom Allâh curses, you will not find for him (any) helper, (52) Or have they a share in the dominion? Then in that case they would not give mankind even a speck on the back of a date-stone. (53) Or do they envy men (Muhammad and his followers) for what Allâh has given them of His Bounty? Then We had already given the family of Ibrâhim (Abraham) the Book and Al¬Hikmah (As¬Sunnah - Divine Revelation to those Prophets not written in the form of a book), and conferred upon them a great kingdom (54) Of them were (some) who believed in him (Muhammad), and of them were (some) who averted their faces from him (Muhammad); and enough is Hell for burning (them). (55) Surely! Those who disbelieved in Our Ayât (proofs, evidences, verses, lessons, signs, revelations, etc.) We shall burn them in Fire. As often as their skins are roasted through, We shall change them for other skins that they may taste the punishment. Truly, Allâh is Ever Most Powerful, All¬Wise. (56) But those who believe (in the Oneness of Allâh - Islâmic Monotheism) and do deeds of righteousness, We shall admit them to Gardens under which rivers flow (Paradise), abiding therein forever. Therein they shall have Azwâjun Mutahharatun [purified mates or wives] and We shall admit them to shades wide and ever deepening (Paradise).

Quran 4:115-123

And whoever contradicts and opposes the Messenger (Muhammad) after the right path has been shown clearly to him, and follows other than the believers' way. We shall keep him in the path he has chosen, and burn him in Hell - what an evil destination. (115) Verily! Allâh forgives not (the sin of) setting up partners (in worship) with Him, but He forgives whom He wills sins other than that, and whoever sets up partners in worship with Allâh, has indeed strayed far away. (116) They (all those who worship others than Allâh) invoke nothing but female deities besides Him (Allâh), and they invoke nothing but Shaitân (Satan), a persistent rebel! (117) Allâh cursed him. And he [Shaitân

(Satan)] said: "I will take an appointed portion of your slaves; (118) Verily, I will mislead them, and surely, I will arouse in them false desires; and certainly, I will order them to slit the ears of cattle, and indeed I will order them to change the nature created by Allâh." And whoever takes Shaitân (Satan) as a Walî (protector or helper) instead of Allâh, has surely suffered a manifest loss.[] (119) He [Shaitan (Satan)] makes promises to them, and arouses in them false desires; and Shaitan's (Satan) promises are nothing but deceptions. (120) The dwelling of such (people) is Hell, and they will find no way of escape from it. (121) But those who believe (in the Oneness of Allâh - Islâmic Monotheism) and do deeds of righteousness, We shall admit them to the Gardens under which rivers flow (i.e. in Paradise) to dwell therein forever. Allâh's Promise is the Truth, and whose words can be truer than those of Allâh? (Of course, none). (122) It will not be in accordance with your desires (Muslims), nor those of the people of the Scripture (Jews and Christians), whosoever works evil, will have the recompense thereof, and he will not find any protector or helper besides Allâh.

Quran 4:136

O you who believe! Believe in Allâh, and His Messenger (Muhammad), and the Book (the Qur'ân) which He has sent down to His Messenger, and the Scripture which He sent down to those before (him), and whosoever disbelieves in Allâh, His Angels, His Books, His Messengers, and the Last Day, then indeed he has strayed far away

Quran 4:150-175

Verily, those who disbelieve in Allâh and His Messengers and wish to make distinction between Allâh and His Messengers (by believing in Allâh and disbelieving in His Messengers) saying,

"We believe in some but reject others," and wish to adopt a way in between. (150) They are in truth disbelievers. And We have prepared for the disbelievers a humiliating torment. (151) And those who believe in Allâh and His Messengers and make no distinction between any of them (Messengers), We shall give them their rewards, and Allâh is Ever Oft¬Forgiving, Most Merciful. (152) The people of the Scripture (Jews) ask you to cause a book to descend upon them from heaven. Indeed they asked Mûsa (Moses) for even greater than that, when they said: "Show us Allâh in public," but they were struck with thunderclap and lightning for their wickedness. Then they worshipped the calf even after clear proofs, evidences, and signs had come to them. (Even) so We forgave them. And We gave Mûsa (Moses) a clear proof of authority. (153) And for their covenant, We raised over them the Mount and (on the other occasion) We said: "Enter the gate prostrating (or bowing) with humility;" and We commanded them: "Transgress not (by doing worldly works) on the Sabbath (Saturday)." And We took from them a firm covenant. (154) Because of their breaking the covenant, and of their rejecting the Ayât (proofs, evidences, verses, lessons, signs, revelations, etc.) of Allâh, and of their killing the Prophets unjustly, and of their saying: "Our hearts are wrapped (with coverings, i.e. we do not understand what the Messengers say)" - nay, Allâh has set a seal upon their hearts because of their disbelief, so they believe not but a little. (155) And because of their (Jews) disbelief and uttering against Maryam (Mary) a grave false charge (that she has committed illegal sexual intercourse); (156) And because of their saying (in boast), "We killed Messiah 'Îsā (Jesus), son of Maryam (Mary), the Messenger of Allâh," - but they killed him not, nor crucified him, but the resemblance of 'Îsā (Jesus) was put over another man (and they killed that man), and those who differ therein are full of doubts. They have no (certain) knowledge, they

follow nothing but conjecture. For surely; they killed him not [i.e.
'Īsā (Jesus), son of Maryam (Mary)]: (157) But Allâh raised him
['Īsā (Jesus)] up (with his body and soul) unto Himself (and he is
in the heavens). And Allâh is Ever All-Powerful, All-Wise. (158)
And there is none of the people of the Scripture (Jews and
Christians), but must believe in him ['Īsā (Jesus), son of Maryam
(Mary), as only a Messenger of Allâh and a human being], before
his ['Īsā (Jesus) or a Jew's or a Christian's] death (at the time of
the appearance of the angel of death). And on the Day of
Resurrection, he ['Īsā (Jesus)] will be a witness against them (159)
For the wrong-doing of the Jews, We made unlawful for them
certain good foods which has been lawful for them, and for their
hindering many from Allâh's Way; (160) And their taking of Ribâ
(usury/interest) though they were forbidden from taking it and
their devouring of men's substance wrongfully (bribery). And We
have prepared for the disbelievers among them a painful torment.
(161) But those among them who are well-grounded in knowledge,
and the believers, believe in what has been sent down to you
(Muhammad) and what was sent down before you, and those who
perform As-Salât, and give Zakât and believe in Allâh and in the
Last Day, it is they to whom We shall give a great reward. (162)
Verily, We have sent the revelation to you (O Muhammad) as We
sent the revelation to Nûh (Noah) and the Prophets after him; We
(also) sent the revelation to Ibrâhîm (Abraham), Ismâ'îl (Ishmael),
Ishâq (Isaac), Ya'qûb (Jacob), and Al-Asbât [the offspring of the
twelve sons of Ya'qûb (Jacob)], 'Īsâ (Jesus), Ayyûb (Job), Yûnus
(Jonah), Hârûn (Aaron), and Sulaimân (Solomon); and to Dâwûd
(David) We gave the Zabûr. (163) And Messengers We have
mentioned to you before, and Messengers We have not mentioned
to you, - and to Mûsa (Moses) Allâh spoke directly. (164)
Messengers as bearers of good news as well as of warning in order
that mankind should have no plea against Allâh after the (coming

of) Messengers. And Allâh is Ever All-Powerful, All-Wise. (165) But Allâh bears witness to that which He has sent down (the Qur'ân) unto you (O Muhammad), He has sent it down with His Knowledge, and the angels bear witness. And Allâh is All-Sufficient as a Witness. (166) Verily, those who disbelieve [by concealing the truth about Prophet Muhammad and his message of true Islâmic Monotheism written in the Taurât (Torah) and the Injeel with them] and prevent (mankind) from the Path of Allâh (Islâmic Monotheism), they have certainly strayed far away. (167) Verily, those who disbelieve and did wrong [by concealing the truth about Prophet Muhammad and his message of true Islâmic Monotheism written in the Taurât (Torah) and the Injeel (Gospel) with them], Allâh will not forgive them, nor will He guide them to any way, - (168) Except the way of Hell, to dwell therein forever, and this is ever easy for Allâh. (169) O mankind! Verily, there has come to you the Messenger (Muhammad) with the truth from your Lord, so believe in him, it is better for you. But if you disbelieve, then certainly to Allâh belongs all that is in the heavens and the earth. And Allâh is Ever All-Knowing, All-Wise. (170) O people of the Scripture! Do not exceed the limits in your religion, nor say of Allâh aught but the truth. The Messiah Īsā(Jesus), son of Maryam (Mary), was (no more than) a Messenger of Allâh and His Word, ("Be!" - and he was) which He bestowed on Maryam (Mary) and a spirit (Rûh) created by Him; so believe in Allâh and His Messengers. Say not: "Three (trinity)!" Cease! (it is) better for you. For Allâh is (the only) One Ilâh (God), glory be to Him (Far Exalted is He) above having a son. To Him belongs all that is in the heavens and all that is in the earth. And Allâh is All¬Sufficient as a Disposer of affairs. (171) The Messiah will never be proud to reject to be a slave of Allâh, nor the angels who are near (to Allâh). And whosoever rejects His worship and is proud, then He will gather them all together unto Himself. (172) So, as for those who believed (in the Oneness of Allâh - Islâmic Monotheism) and did deeds of righteousness, He will give their (due) rewards, and more out of His Bounty. But as for those who refused His worship and were proud, He will punish them with a painful torment . And they will not find for themselves besides Allâh any protector or helper. (173) O mankind! Verily, there has come to you a convincing proof (Prophet Muhammad) from your Lord, and We sent down to you a manifest light (this Qur'ân). (174) So, as for those who believed in Allâh and held fast to Him, He will admit them to His Mercy and Grace (i.e. Paradise), and guide them to Himself by a Straight Path.

Quran 5:10

And those who disbelieve and deny our Ayât (proofs, evidences, verses, lessons, signs, revelations, etc.) are those who will be the dwellers of the Hell-fire.

Quran 5:12-19

Indeed Allâh took the covenant from the Children of Israel (Jews), and We appointed twelve leaders among them. And Allâh said: "I am with you if you perform As-Salât and give Zakât and believe in My Messengers; honour and assist them, and lend a good loan to Allâh. Verily, I will expiate your sins and admit you to Gardens under which rivers flow (in Paradise). But if any of you after this, disbelieved, he has indeed gone astray from the Straight Path." (12) So because of their breach of their covenant, We cursed them, and made their hearts grow hard. They change the words from their (right) places and have abandoned a good part of the Message that was sent to them. And you will not cease to discover deceit in them, except a few of them. But forgive them, and overlook (their misdeeds). Verily, Allâh loves Al¬Muhsinûn (good¬doers). (13) And from those who call themselves Christians, We took their covenant, but they have abandoned a good part of the Message that was sent to them. So We planted amongst them enmity and hatred till the Day of Resurrection (when they discarded Allâh's Book, disobeyed Allâh's Messengers and His Orders and transgressed beyond bounds in Allâh's disobedience), and Allâh will inform them of what they used to do. (14) O people of the Scripture (Jews and Christians)! Now has come to you Our Messenger (Muhammad) explaining to you much of that which you used to hide from the Scripture and pass over (i.e. leaving out without explaining) much. Indeed, there has come to you from Allâh a light (Prophet Muhammad) and a plain Book (this Qur'ân). (15) Wherewith Allâh guides all those who seek His Good Pleasure to ways of peace, and He brings them out of darkness by His Will unto light and guides them to a Straight Way (Islâmic Monotheism) (16) Surely, in disbelief are they who say that Allâh is the Messiah, son of Maryam (Mary). Say: "Who then has the least power against Allâh, if He were to destroy the Messiah, son of Maryam (Mary), his mother, and all those who are on the earth together?" And to Allâh belongs the dominion of the heavens and the earth, and all that is between them. He creates what He wills. And Allâh is Able to do all things. (17) And (both) the Jews and the Christians say: "We are the children of Allâh and His loved ones." Say: "Why then does He punish you for your sins?" Nay, you are but human beings, of those He has created, He forgives whom He wills and He punishes whom He wills. And to Allâh belongs the dominion of the heavens and the earth and all that is between them, and to Him is the return (of all). (18) O people of the Scripture (Jews and Christians)! Now has come to you Our Messenger (Muhammad) making (things) clear unto you, after a break in (the series of) Messengers, lest you say: "There came unto us no bringer of glad tidings and no warner." But now has come unto you a bringer of glad tidings and a warner. And Allâh is Able to do all things.

Quran 5:41-51

O Messenger (Muhammad)! Let not those who hurry to fall into disbelief grieve you, of such who say: "We believe" with their mouths but their hearts have no faith. And of the Jews are men who listen much and eagerly to lies - listen to others who have not come to you. They change the words from their places; they say, "If you are given this, take it, but if you are not given this, then beware!" And whomsoever Allâh wants to put in Al¬Fitnah [error, because of his rejecting the Faith], you can do nothing for him against Allâh. Those are the ones whose hearts Allâh does not want to purify (from disbelief and hypocrisy); for them there is a disgrace in this world, and in the Hereafter a great torment. (41) (They like to) listen to falsehood, to devour anything forbidden. So if they come to you (O Muhammad), either judge between them, or turn away from them. If you turn away from them, they cannot hurt you in the least. And if you judge, judge with justice between them. Verily, Allâh loves those who act justly. (42) But how do they come to you for decision while they have the Taurât (Torah), in which is the (plain) Decision of Allâh; yet even after that, they turn away. For they are not (really) believers. (43) Verily, We did send down the Taurât (Torah) [to Mûsa (Moses)], therein was guidance and light, by which the Prophets, who submitted themselves to Allâh's Will, judged for the Jews. And the rabbis and the priests [too judged for the Jews by the Taurât (Torah) after those Prophets] for to them was entrusted the protection of Allâh's Book, and they were witnesses thereto. Therefore fear not men but fear Me (O Jews) and sell not My Verses for a miserable price. And whosoever does not judge by what Allâh has revealed, such are the Kâfirûn (i.e. disbelievers - of a lesser degree as they do not act on

Allâh's Laws). (44) And We ordained therein for them: "Life for life, eye for eye, nose for nose, ear for ear, tooth for tooth, and wounds equal for equal." But if anyone remits the retaliation by way of charity, it shall be for him an expiation. And whosoever does not judge by that which Allâh has revealed, such are the Zâlimûn (polytheists and wrong¬doers - of a lesser degree). (45) And in their footsteps, We sent 'Īsā (Jesus), son of Maryam (Mary), confirming the Taurât (Torah) that had come before him, and We gave him the Injeel, in which was guidance and light and confirmation of the Taurât (Torah) that had come before it, a guidance and an admonition for Al-Muttaqûn (the pious). (46) Let the people of the Injeel judge by what Allâh has revealed therein. And whosoever does not judge by what Allâh has revealed (then) such (people) are the Fâsiqûn (the rebellious i.e. disobedient (of a lesser degree) to Allâh. (47) And We have sent down to you (O Muhammad) the Book (this Qur'ân) in truth, confirming the Scripture that came before it and Muhaymin (trustworthy in highness and a witness) over it (old Scriptures). So judge among them by what Allâh has revealed, and follow not their vain desires, diverging away from the truth that has come to you. To each among you, We have prescribed a law and a clear way. If Allâh had willed, He would have made you one nation, but that (He) may test you in what He has given you; so compete in good deeds. The return of you (all) is to Allâh; then He will inform you about that in which you used to differ (48) And so judge (you O Muhammad) among them by what Allâh has revealed and follow not their vain desires, but beware of them lest they turn you (O Muhammad) far away from some of that which Allâh has sent down to you. And if they turn away, then know that Allâh's Will is to punish them for some sins of theirs. And truly, most of men are Fâsiqûn (rebellious and disobedient to Allâh). (49) Do they then seek the judgement of (the days of) Ignorance? And who is better in judgement than

Allâh for a people who have firm Faith. (50) O you who believe! Take not the Jews and the Christians as Auliyâ' (friends, protectors, helpers), they are but Auliyâ' of each other. And if any amongst you takes them (as Auliyâ'), then surely he is one of them. Verily, Allâh guides not those people who are the Zâlimûn (polytheists and wrong-doers and unjust).

Quran 5:58-81

And when you proclaim the call for As-Salât [call for the prayer (Adhân)], they take it (but) as a mockery and fun; that is because they are a people who understand not. (58) Say: "O people of the Scripture (Jews and Christians)! Do you criticize us for no other reason than that we believe in Allâh, and in (the revelation) which has been sent down to us and in that which has been sent down before (us), and that most of you are Fâsiqûn [rebellious and disobedient (to Allâh)]?" (59)Say:"Shall I inform you of something worse than that, regarding the recompense from Allâh: those (Jews) who incurred the Curse of Allâh and His Wrath, those of whom (some) He transformed into monkeys and swines, those who worshipped Tâghût (false deities); such are worse in rank (on the Day of Resurrection in the Hell¬fire), and far more astray from the Right Path (in the life of this world)." (60) When they come to you, they say: "We believe." But in fact they enter with (an intention of) disbelief and they go out with the same. And Allâh knows all what they were hiding (61) And you see many of them (Jews) hurrying towards sin and transgression, and eating illegal things [as bribes and Ribâ (usury), etc.]. Evil indeed is that which they have been doing (62) Why do not the rabbis and the religious learned men forbid them from uttering sinful words and from eating illegal things. Evil indeed is that which they have been performing. (63) The Jews say: "Allâh's Hand is tied up (i.e. He does not give and spend of His Bounty)." Be their hands tied up and be they accursed for what they uttered. Nay, both His Hands are widely outstretched. He spends (of His Bounty) as He wills. Verily, the Revelation that has come to you from your Lord (Allâh) increases in most of them (their) obstinate rebellion and disbelief. We have put enmity and hatred amongst them till the Day of Resurrection. Every time they kindled the fire of war, Allâh extinguished it; and they (ever) strive to make mischief on earth. And Allâh does not like the Mufsidûn (mischief-makers). (64) And if only the people of the Scripture (Jews and Christians) had believed (in Muhammad) and warded off evil (sin, ascribing partners to Allâh) and had become Al¬Muttaqûn (the pious) We would indeed have expiated from them their sins and admitted them to Gardens of pleasure (in Paradise). (65) And if only they had acted according to the Taurât (Torah), the Injeel, and what has (now) been sent down to them from their Lord (the Qur'ân), they would surely have gotten provision from above them and from underneath their feet. There are from among them people who are on the right course (i.e. they act on the revelation and believe in Prophet Muhammad as 'Abdullâh bin Salâm did), but many of them do evil deeds. (66) O Messenger (Muhammad)! Proclaim (the Message) which has been sent down to you from your Lord. And if you do not, then you have not conveyed His Message. Allâh will protect you from mankind. Verily, Allâh guides not the people who disbelieve. (67) Say "O people of the Scripture (Jews and Christians)! You have nothing (as regards guidance) till you act according to the Taurât (Torah), the Injeel, and what has (now) been sent down to you from your Lord (the Qur'ân)." Verily, that which has been sent down to you (Muhammad) from your Lord increases in most of them (their) obstinate rebellion and disbelief. So be not sorrowful over the people who disbelieve. (68) Surely, those who believe (in the Oneness of Allâh, in His Messenger Muhammad and all that was revealed to him from Allâh), those who are the Jews and the Sabians and the Christians, - whosoever believed in Allâh and the Last Day, and worked righteousness, on them shall be no fear, nor shall they grieve. (69) Verily, We took the covenant of the Children of Israel and sent Messengers to them. Whenever there came to them a Messenger with what they themselves desired not - a group of them they called liars, and others among them they killed. (70) They thought there will be no Fitnah (trial or punishment), so they became blind and deaf; after that Allâh turned to them (with Forgiveness); yet again many of them became blind and deaf. And Allâh is the All¬Seer of what they do. (71) Surely, they have disbelieved who say: "Allâh is the Messiah Īsā (Jesus), son of Maryam (Mary)." But the Messiah Īsā(Jesus) said: "O Children of Israel! Worship Allâh, my Lord and your Lord." Verily, whosoever sets up partners (in worship) with Allâh, then Allâh has forbidden Paradise to him, and the Fire will be his abode. And for the Zâlimûn (polytheists and wrong-doers) there are no helpers (72) Surely, disbelievers are those who said: "Allâh is the third of the three (in a Trinity)." But there is no llâh (god) (none who has the right to be worshipped) but One Ilâh (God -Allâh). And if they cease not from what they say, verily, a painful torment will befall on the disbelievers among them (73) Will they not turn with repentance to Allâh and ask His Forgiveness? For Allâh is Oft-Forgiving, Most Merciful. (74) The Messiah ['Īsā (Jesus)], son of Maryam (Mary), was no more than a Messenger; many were the Messengers that passed away before him. His mother [Maryam (Mary)] was a Siddiqah [i.e. she believed in the words of Allâh and His Books]. They both used to eat food (as any other human being, while Allâh does not eat). Look how We make the Ayât (proofs, evidences, verses, lessons, signs, revelations, etc.) clear to them, yet look how they are deluded away (from the truth) (75) Say: "How do you worship besides Allâh something which has no power either to harm or to benefit you? But it is Allâh Who is the All¬Hearer, All¬Knower." (76) Say: "O people of the Scripture (Jews and Christians)! Exceed not the limits in your religion (by believing in something) other than the truth, and do not follow the vain desires of people who went astray before, and who misled many, and strayed (themselves) from the Right Path." (77) Those among the Children of Israel who disbelieved were cursed by the tongue of Dawûd (David) and 'Īsā (Jesus), son of Maryam (Mary). That was because they disobeyed (Allâh and the Messengers) and were ever transgressing beyond bounds. (78) They used not to forbid one another from Al-Munkar (wrong, evil-doing, sins, polytheism, disbelief) which they committed. Vile indeed was what they used to do. (79) You see many of them taking the disbelievers as their Auliyâ' (protectors and helpers). Evil indeed is that which their ownselves have sent forward before them, for that (reason) Allâh's Wrath fell upon them and in torment they will abide. (80) And had they believed in Allâh, and in the Prophet (Muhammad) and in what has been revealed to him, never would they have taken them (the disbelievers) as Auliyâ' (protectors and helpers), but many of them are the Fâsiqûn (rebellious, disobedient to Allâh).

Quran 5:109-119

On the Day when Allâh will gather the Messengers together and say to them: "What was the response you received (from men to your teaching)? They will say: "We have no knowledge, verily, only You are the All¬Knower of all that is hidden (or unseen)." (109) (Remember) when Allâh will say (on the Day of Resurrection). "O 'Īsā (Jesus), son of Maryam (Mary)! Remember My Favour to you and to your mother when I supported you with Rûh-ul-Qudus [Jibrail (Gabriel)] so that you spoke to the people in the cradle and in maturity; and when I taught you writing, Al¬Hikmah (the power of understanding), the Taurât (Torah) and the Injeel (Gospel); and when you made out of the clay, a figure like that of a bird, by My Permission, and you breathed into it, and it became a bird by My Permission, and you healed those born blind, and the lepers by My Permission, and when you brought forth the dead by My Permission; and when I restrained the Children of Israel from you (when they resolved to kill you) as you came unto them with clear proofs, and the disbelievers among them said: 'This is nothing but evident magic.' " (110) And when I (Allâh) revealed Al-Hawârîyyun (the disciples) [of 'Īsā (Jesus)] to believe in Me and My Messenger, they said: "We believe. And bear witness that we are Muslims." (111) (Remember) when Al-Hawârîyyûn (the disciples) said: "O 'Īsā (Jesus), son of Maryam (Mary)! Can your Lord send down to us a table spread (with food) from heaven?" 'Īsā (Jesus) said: "Fear Allâh, if you are indeed believers." (112) They said: "We wish to eat thereof and to satisfy your heart (to be stronger in Faith), and to know that you have indeed told us the truth and that we ourselves be its witnesses." (113) 'Īsā (Jesus), son of Maryam (Mary), said: "O Allâh, our Lord! Send us from heaven a table spread (with food) that there may be for us - for the first and the last of us - a festival and a sign from You; and provide us sustenance, for You are the Best of sustainers." (114) Allâh said: "I am going to send it down unto you, but if any of you after that disbelieves, then I will punish him with a torment such as I have not inflicted on anyone among (all) the 'Alamîn (mankind and jinn)." (115) And (remember) when Allâh will say (on the Day of Resurrection): "O 'Īsā (Jesus), son of Maryam (Mary)! Did you say unto men: 'Worship me and my mother as two gods besides Allâh?' " He will say: "Glory be to You! It was not for me to say what I had no right (to say). Had I said such a thing, You would surely have known it. You know what is in my inner-self though I do not know what is in Yours, truly, You, only You, are the All-Knower of all that is hidden (and unseen). (116) "Never did I say to them aught except what You (Allâh) did command me to say: 'Worship Allâh, my Lord and your Lord.' And I was a witness over them while I dwelt amongst them, but when You took me up, You were the Watcher over them, and You are a Witness to all things. (117) "If You punish them, they are Your slaves, and if You forgive them, verily You, only You are the All¬Mighty, the All¬Wise." (118) Allâh will say: "This is a Day on which the truthful will profit from their truth: theirs are Gardens under which rivers flow (in Paradise) - they shall abide therein forever. Allâh is pleased with them and they with Him. That is the great success (Paradise).

Quran 6:1

All praises and thanks be to Allâh, Who (Alone) created the heavens and the earth, and originated the darkness and the light, yet those who disbelieve hold others as equal with their Lord.

Quran 6:20-28

Those to whom We have given the Scripture (Jews and Christians) recognize him (i.e. Muhammad as a Messenger of Allâh, and they also know that there is no Ilah (God) but Allâh and Islâm is Allâh's religion), as they recognize their own sons. Those who have lost (destroyed) themselves will not believe. (20) And who does more wrong and aggression than he who invents a lie against Allâh or rejects His Ayât (proofs, evidences, verses, lessons, or revelations)? Verily, the Zâlimûn (polytheists and wrong-doers,) shall never be successful. (21) And on the Day when We shall gather them all together, We shall say to those who joined partners (in worship with Us): "Where are your partners (false deities) whom you used to assert (as partners in worship with Allâh)?" (22) There will then be (left) no Fitnah (excuses or statements or arguments) for them but to say: "By Allâh, our Lord, we were not those who joined others in worship with Allâh." (23) Look! How they lie against themselves! But the (lie) which they invented will disappear from them. (24) And of them there are some who listen to you; but We have set veils on their hearts, so they understand it not, and deafness in their ears; and even if they see every one of the Ayât (proofs, evidences, verses, lessons, signs, revelations, etc.) they will not believe therein; to the point that when they come to you to argue with you, the disbelievers say: "These are nothing but tales of the men of old." (25) And they prevent others from him (from following Prophet Muhammad) and they themselves keep away from him, and (by doing so) they destroy not but their ownselves, yet they perceive (it) not. (26) If you could but see when they will be held over the (Hell) Fire! They will say: "Would that we were but sent back (to the world)! Then we would not deny the Ayât (proofs, evidences, verses, lessons, revelations, etc.) of our Lord, and we would be of the believers!" (27) Nay, it has become manifest to them what they had been concealing before. But if they were returned (to the world), they would certainly revert to that which they were forbidden. And indeed they are liars.

Quran 6:91-94

They (the Jews, Quraish pagans, idolaters) did not estimate Allâh with an estimation due to Him when they said: "Nothing did Allâh send down to any human being (by revelation)." Say (O Muhammad): "Who then sent down the Book which Mûsa (Moses) brought, a light and a guidance to mankind which you (the Jews) have made into (separate) papersheets, disclosing (some of it) and concealing much. And you (believers in Allâh and His Messenger Muhammad), were taught (through the Qur'ân) that which neither you nor your fathers knew." Say: "Allâh (sent it down)." Then leave them to play in their vain discussions. (91) And this (the Qur'ân) is a blessed Book which We have sent down,

[45]

confirming (the revelations) which came before it, so that you may warn the Mother of Towns (i.e. Makkah) and all those around it. Those who believe in the Hereafter believe in it (the Qur'ân), and they are constant in guarding their Salât (prayers). (92) And who can be more unjust than he who invents a lie against Allâh, or says: "A revelation has come to me," whereas as no revelation has come to him in anything; and who says, "I will reveal the like of what Allâh has revealed." And if you could but see when the Zâlimûn (polytheists and wrong-doers) are in the agonies of death, while the angels are stretching forth their hands (saying): "Deliver your souls! This day you shall be recompensed with the torment of degradation because of what you used to utter against Allâh other than the truth. And you used to reject His Ayât (proofs, evidences, verses, lessons, signs, revelations etc.) with disrespect!" (93) And truly you have come unto Us alone (without wealth, companions or anything else) as We created you the first time. You have left behind you all that which We had bestowed on you. We see not with you your intercessors whom you claimed to be partners with Allâh. Now all relations between you and them have been cut off, and all that you used to claim has vanished from you.

Quran 6:101-103

He is the Originator of the heavens and the earth. How can He have children when He has no wife? He created all things and He is the All-Knower of everything (101) Such is Allâh, your Lord! Lâ ilâha illa Huwa (none has the right to be worshipped but He), the Creator of all things. So worship Him (Alone), and He is the Wakîl (Trustee, Disposer of affairs, Guardian) over all things. (102) No vision can grasp Him, but He grasps all vision. He is Al-Latif (the Most Subtle and Courteous), Well-Acquainted with all things.

Quran 6:114

[Say (O Muhammad)] "Shall I seek a judge other than Allâh while it is He Who has sent down unto you the Book (the Qur'ân), explained in detail." Those unto whom We gave the Scripture [the Taurât (Torah) and the Injeel] know that it is revealed from your Lord in truth. So be not you of those who doubt.

Quran 6:146-155

And unto those who are Jews, We forbade every (animal) with undivided hoof, and We forbade them the fat of the ox and the sheep except what adheres to their backs or their entrails, or is mixed up with a bone. Thus We recompensed them for their rebellion [committing crimes like murdering the Prophets, eating of Ribâ (usury)]. And verily, We are Truthful. (146) If they (Jews) belie you (Muhammad) say: "Your Lord is the Owner of Vast Mercy, and never will His Wrath be turned back from the people who are Mujrimûn (criminals, polytheists, or sinners)." (147) Those who took partners (in worship) with Allâh will say: "If Allâh had willed, we would not have taken partners (in worship) with Him, nor would our fathers, and we would not have forbidden anything (against His Will)." Likewise belied those who were before them, (they argued falsely with Allâh's Messengers), till they tasted Our Wrath. Say: "Have you any knowledge (proof) that you can produce before us? Verily, you follow nothing but guess and you do nothing but lie." (148) Say: "With Allâh is the perfect proof and argument, (i.e. the Oneness of Allâh, the sending of His Messengers and His Books to mankind), had He so willed, He would indeed have guided you all." (149) Say: "Bring forward your witnesses, who can testify that Allâh has forbidden this. Then if they testify, testify not you (O Muhammad) with them. And you should not follow the vain desires of such as treat Our Ayât (proofs, evidences, verses, lessons, signs, revelations, etc.) as falsehoods, and such as believe not in the Hereafter, and they hold others as equal (in worship) with their Lord." (150) Say (O Muhammad): "Come, I will recite what your Lord has prohibited you from: Join not anything in worship with Him; be good and dutiful to your parents; kill not your children because of poverty - We provide sustenance for you and for them; come not near to Al-Fawâhish (shameful sins, illegal sexual intercourse,) whether committed openly or secretly, and kill not anyone whom Allâh has forbidden, except for a just cause (according to Islâmic law). This He has commanded you that you may understand. (151) "And come not near to the orphan's property, except to improve it, until he (or she) attains the age of full strength; and give full measure and full weight with justice. We burden not any person, but that which he can bear. And whenever you give your word (i.e. judge between men or give evidence), say the truth even if a near relative is concerned, and fulfill the Covenant of Allâh, This He commands you, that you may remember. (152) "And verily, this (i.e. Allâh's Commandments mentioned in the above two Verses 151 and 152) is my Straight Path, so follow it, and follow not (other) paths, for they will separate you away from His Path. This He has ordained for you that you may become Al-Muttaqûn (the pious)." (153) Then, We gave Mûsa (Moses) the Book [the Taurât (Torah)], to complete (Our Favour) upon those who would do right, and explaining all things in detail and a guidance and a mercy that they might believe in the meeting with their Lord. (154) And this is a blessed Book (the Qur'ân) which We have sent down, so follow it and fear Allâh (i.e. do not disobey His Orders), that you may receive mercy (i.e. be saved from the torment of Hell).

Quran 7:37

Who is more unjust than one who invents a lie against Allâh or rejects His Ayât (proofs, evidences, verses, lessons, signs, revelations)? For such their appointed portion (good things of this worldly life and their period of stay therein) will reach them from the Book (of Decrees) until, when Our Messengers (the angel of death and his assistants) come to them to take their souls, they (the angels) will say: "Where are those whom you used to invoke and worship besides Allâh," they will reply, "They have vanished and deserted us." And they will bear witness against themselves, that they were disbelievers.

Quran 8:2-4

The believers are only those who, when Allâh is mentioned, feel a fear in their hearts and when His Verses (this Qur'ân) are recited unto them, they (i.e. the Verses) increase their Faith; and they put their trust in their Lord (Alone); (2) Who perform As-Salât and spend out of that We have provided them. (3) It is they who are the believers in truth. For them are grades of dignity with their Lord, and Forgiveness and a generous provision (Paradise).

Quran 9:28-35

O you who believe (in Allâh's Oneness and in His Messenger (Muhammad)! Verily, the Mushrikûn (polytheists, pagans, idolaters, disbelievers in the Oneness of Allâh, and in the Message of Muhammad) are Najasun (impure). So let them not come near Al-Masjid-al-Harâm (at Makkah) after this year, and if you fear poverty, Allâh will enrich you if He wills, out of His Bounty. Surely, Allâh is All-Knowing, All-Wise. (28) Fight against those who (1) believe not in Allâh, (2) nor in the Last Day, (3) nor forbid that which has been forbidden by Allâh and His Messenger (Muhammad) (4) and those who acknowledge not the religion of truth (i.e. Islâm) among the people of the Scripture (Jews and Christians), until they pay the Jizyah with willing submission, and feel themselves subdued. (29) And the Jews say: 'Uzair (Ezra) is the son of Allâh, and the Christians say: Messiah is the son of

[49]

Allâh. That is their saying with their mouths, resembling the saying of the those who disbelieved aforetime. Allâh's Curse be on them, how they are deluded away from the truth!(30) They (Jews and Christians) took their rabbis and their monks to be their lords besides Allâh (by obeying them in things which they made lawful or unlawful according to their own desires without being ordered by Allâh), and (they also took as their Lord) Messiah, son of Maryam (Mary), while they (Jews and Christians) were commanded [in the Taurât (Torah) and the Injeel) to worship none but One Ilâh (God - Allâh) Lâ ilâha illa Huwa (none has the right to be worshipped but He). Praise and glory is to Him, (far above is He) from having the partners they associate (with Him)." (31) They (the disbelievers, the Jews and the Christians) want to extinguish Allâh's Light (with which Muhammad has been sent - Islâmic Monotheism) with their mouths, but Allâh will not allow except that His Light should be perfected even though the Kâfirûn (disbelievers) hate (it). (32) It is He Who has sent His Messenger (Muhammad) with guidance and the religion of truth (Islâm), to make it superior over all religions even though the Mushrikûn (polytheists, pagans, idolaters, disbelievers in the Oneness of Allâh) hate (it). (33) O you who believe! Verily, there are many of the (Jewish) rabbis and the (Christian) monks who devour the wealth of mankind in falsehood, and hinder (them) from the Way of Allâh (i.e. Allâh's religion of Islâmic Monotheism). And those who hoard up gold and silver [Al-Kanz: the money, the Zakât of which has not been paid], and spend them not in the Way of Allâh, - announce unto them a painful torment. (34) On the Day when that (Al-Kanz: money, gold and silver, the Zakât of which has not been paid) will be heated in the Fire of Hell and with it will be branded their foreheads, their flanks, and their backs, (and it will be said unto them):-"This is the treasure which you hoarded for yourselves. Now taste of what you used to hoard."

Quran 9:63

*Know they not that whoever opposes and shows hostility to Allâh
and His Messenger, certainly for him will be the Fire of Hell to
abide therein. That is extreme disgrace.*

Quran 9:113

*It is not (proper) for the Prophet and those who believe to ask
Allâh's Forgiveness for the Mushrikûn (polytheists, idolaters,
pagans, disbelievers in the Oneness of Allâh) even though they be
of kin, after it has become clear to them that they are the dwellers of
the Fire.*

Quran 10:17-19

*So who does more wrong than he who forges a lie against Allâh or
denies His Ayât (proofs, evidences, verses, lessons, signs,
revelations, etc.)? Surely, the Mujrimûn (criminals, sinners,
disbelievers and polytheists) will never be successful! (17) And
they worship besides Allâh things that hurt them not, nor profit
them, and they say: "These are our intercessors with Allâh." Say:
"Do you inform Allâh of that which He knows not in the heavens
and on the earth?" Glorified and Exalted is He above all that which
they associate as partners (with Him)! (18) Mankind were but one
community (i.e. on one religion - Islâmic Monotheism), then they
differed (later), and had not it been for a Word that went forth
before from your Lord, it would have been settled between them
regarding what they differed*

Quran 10:28-39

*And the Day whereon We shall gather them all together, then We
shall say to those who did set partners in worship with Us: "Stop
at your place! You and your partners (whom you had worshipped*

in the worldly life)." then We shall separate them, and their (Allâh's so-called) partners shall say: "It was not us that you used to worship." (28) "So sufficient is Allâh for a witness between us and you, that We indeed knew nothing of your worship of us." (29) There! Every person will know (exactly) what he had earned before, and they will be brought back to Allâh, their rightful Maula (Lord), and their invented false deities will vanish from them. (30) Say (O Muhammad): "Who provides for you from the sky and the earth? Or who owns hearing and sight? And who brings out the living from the dead and brings out the dead from the living? And who disposes the affairs?" They will say: "Allâh." Say: "Will you not then be afraid of Allâh's Punishment (for setting up rivals in worship with Allâh)?" (31) Such is Allâh, your Lord in truth. So after the truth, what else can there be, save error? How then are you turned away? (32) Thus is the Word of your Lord justified against those who rebel (disobey Allâh) that they will not believe (in the Oneness of Allâh and in Muhammad as the Messenger of Allâh) (33) Say: "Is there of your (Allâh's so-called) partners one that originates the creation and then repeats it?" Say: "Allâh originates the creation and then He repeats it. Then how are you deluded away (from the truth)?" (34) Say: "Is there of your (Allâh's so-called) partners one that guides to the truth?" Say: "It is Allâh Who guides to the truth. Is then He, Who guides to the truth, more worthy to be followed, or he who finds not guidance (himself) unless he is guided? Then, what is the matter with you? How judge you?" (35) And most of them follow nothing but conjecture. Certainly, conjecture can be of no avail against the truth. Surely, Allâh is All-Aware of what they do. (36) And this Qur'ân is not such as could ever be produced by other than Allâh (Lord of the heavens and the earth), but it is a confirmation of (the revelation) which was before it [i.e. the Taurât (Torah), and the Injeel], and a full explanation of the Book (i.e. laws decreed for

mankind) - wherein there is no doubt from the the Lord of the
'Alamîn (mankind, jinn,and all that exists). (37) Or do they say:
"He (Muhammad) has forged it?" Say: "Bring then a Sûrah
(chapter) like unto it, and call upon whomsoever you can, besides
Allâh, if you are truthful!" (38) Nay, they have belied; the
knowledge whereof they could not comprehend and what has not
yet been fulfilled (i.e. their punishment). Thus those before them
did belie. Then see what was the end of the Zâlimûn (polytheists
and wrong-doers)!

Quran 10:68-70

They (Jews, Christians and pagans) say: "Allâh has begotten a son
(children)." Glory is to Him! He is Rich (Free of all needs). His is
all that is in the heavens and all that is in the earth. No warrant
you have for this. Do you say against Allâh what you know not.
(68) Say: "Verily, those who invent a lie against Allâh will never
be successful" - (69) (A brief) enjoyment in this world! - and then
unto Us will be their return, then We shall make them taste the
severest torment because they used to disbelieve [in Allâh, belie His
Messengers, deny and challenge His Ayât (proofs, signs, verses,)].

Quran 10:106

"And invoke not besides Allâh, any that will neither profit you,
nor hurt you, but if (in case) you did so, you shall certainly be one
of the Zâlimûn (polytheists and wrong-doers)."

Quran 11:17-22

Can they (Muslims) who rely on a clear proof (the Qur'ân) from
their Lord, and whom a witness [Jibrail (Gabriel)] from Him recites
(follows) it (can they be equal with the disbelievers); and before it,
came the Book of Mûsa (Moses), a guidance and a mercy, they
believe therein, but those of the sects (Jews, Christians and all the

other non-Muslim nations) that reject it (the Qur'ân), the Fire will be their promised meeting-place. So be not in doubt about it (i.e. those who denied Prophet Muhammad and also denied all that which he brought from Allâh, surely, they will enter Hell). Verily, it is the truth from your Lord, but most of the mankind believe not (17) And who does more wrong than he who invents a lie against Allâh. Such will be brought before their Lord, and the witnesses will say, "These are the ones who lied against their Lord!" No doubt! the curse of Allâh is on the Zâlimûn (polytheists, wrong-doers, oppressors) (18) Those who hinder (others) from the Path of Allâh (Islâmic Monotheism), and seek a crookedness therein, while they are disbelievers in the Hereafter. (19) By no means will they escape (from Allâh's Torment) on earth, nor have they protectors besides Allâh! Their torment will be doubled! They could not bear to hear (the preachers of the truth) and they used not to see (the truth because of their severe aversion, inspite of the fact that they had the sense of hearing and sight). (20) They are those who have lost their ownselves, and their invented false deities will vanish from them. (21) Certainly, they are those who will be the greatest losers in the Hereafter.

Quran 13:18-19

For those who answered their Lord's Call [believed in the Oneness of Allâh and followed His Messenger Muhammad i.e. Islâmic Monotheism] is Al-Husna (i.e. Paradise). But those who answered not His Call (disbelieved in the Oneness of Allâh and followed not His Messenger Muhammad), if they had all that is in the earth together with its like, they would offer it in order to save themselves (from the torment, but it will be in vain). For them there will be the terrible reckoning. Their dwelling - place will be Hell; - and worst indeed is that place for rest. (18) Shall he then who knows that what has been revealed unto you (O Muhammad) from your Lord is the truth be like him who is blind? But it is only the men of understanding that pay heed.

Quran 13:43

And those who disbelieved, say: "You (O Muhammad) are not a Messenger." Say: "Sufficient as a witness between me and you is Allâh and those too who have knowledge of the Scripture (such as 'Abdullâh bin Salâm, Salman Farsi and other Jews and Christians who embraced Islâm)."

Quran 15:2

How much will those who disbelieve desire that they were Muslims [those who have submitted themselves to Allâh's Will in Islâm i.e. Islâmic Monotheism, this will be on the Day of Resurrection when they will see the disbelievers going to Hell and the Muslims going to Paradise].

Quran 16:35-36

And those who joined others in worship with Allâh say: "If Allâh had so willed, neither we nor our fathers would have worshipped aught but Him, nor would we have forbidden anything without (Command from) Him." So did those before them. Then! Are the Messengers charged with anything but to convey clearly the Message? (35) And verily, We have sent among every Ummah (community, nation) a Messenger (proclaiming): "Worship Allâh (Alone), and avoid (or keep away from) Tâghût (all false deities, etc. i.e. do not worship Tâghût besides Allâh)." Then of them were some whom Allâh guided and of them were some upon whom the straying was justified. So travel through the land and see what was the end of those who denied (the truth).

Quran 16:86-89

And when those who associated partners with Allâh see their (Allâh's so-called) partners, they will say: "Our Lord! These are our partners whom we used to invoke besides you." But they will throw back their word at them (and say): "Surely! You indeed are liars!" (86) And they will offer (their full) submission to Allâh (Alone) on that Day, and their invented false deities [all that they used to invoke besides Allâh, e.g. idols, saints, priests, monks, angels, jinn, Jibrael (Gabriel), Messengers] will vanish from them. (87) Those who disbelieved and hinder (men) from the Path of Allâh, for them We will add torment to the torment; because they used to spread corruption [by disobeying Allâh themselves, as well as ordering others (mankind) to do so]. (88) And (remember) the Day when We shall raise up from every nation a witness against them from amongst themselves. And We shall bring you (O Muhammad) as a witness against these. And We have sent down to you the Book (the Qur'an) as an exposition of everything, a guidance, a mercy, and glad tidings for those who have submitted themselves (to Allâh as Muslims).

Quran 17:56-57

Say: "Call upon those - besides Him - whom you pretend [to be gods like angels, Isâ (Jesus), 'Uzair (Ezra) and others]. They have neither the power to remove the adversity from you nor even to shift it from you to another person." (56) Those whom they call upon [like 'Īsā (Jesus) son of Maryam (Mary), 'Uzair (Ezra), angels] desire (for themselves) means of access to their Lord (Allâh), as to which of them should be the nearest and they ['Īsā (Jesus), 'Uzair (Ezra), angels and others] hope for His Mercy and fear His Torment. Verily, the Torment of your Lord is (something) to be afraid of!

Quran 17:111

And say: "All the praises and thanks are to Allâh, Who has not begotten a son (nor offspring), and Who has no partner in (His) Dominion, nor He is low to have a Walî (helper, protector or supporter). And magnify Him with all the magnificence

Quran 18:4-6

And to warn those (Jews, Christians, and pagans) who say, "Allâh has begotten a son (or offspring or children)." (4) No knowledge have they of such a thing, nor had their fathers. Mighty is the word that comes out of their mouths (i.e. He begot sons and daughters). They utter nothing but a lie. (5) Perhaps, you, would kill yourself in grief, over their footsteps (for their turning away from you), because they believe not in this narration (the Qur'ân).

Quran 18:56-57

And We send not the Messengers except as givers of glad tidings and warners. But those who disbelieve, dispute with false argument, in order to refute the truth thereby. And they treat My Ayât (proofs, evidences, verses, lessons, signs, revelations, etc.), and that with which they are warned, as jest and mockery! (56) And who does more wrong than he who is reminded of the Ayât (proofs, evidences, verses, lessons, signs, revelations, etc.) of his Lord, but turns away from them forgetting what (deeds) his hands have sent forth. Truly, We have set veils over their hearts lest they should understand this (the Qur'ân), and in their ears, deafness. And if you (O Muhammad) call them to guidance, even then they will never be guided.

Quran 18:100-106

And on that Day We shall present Hell to the disbelievers, plain to view, – (100) (To) those whose eyes had been under a covering from My Reminder (this Qur'ân), and who could not bear to hear (it). (101) Do then those who disbelieved think that they can take My slaves [i.e., the angels, Allâh's Messengers, 'Īsā (Jesus), son of Maryam (Mary)] as Auliyâ' (lords, gods, protectors) besides Me? Verily, We have prepared Hell as an entertainment for the disbelievers (in the Oneness of Allâh Islâmic Monotheism). (102) Say (O Muhammad): "Shall We tell you the greatest losers in respect of (their) deeds? (103) "Those whose efforts have been wasted in this life while they thought that they were acquiring good by their deeds! (104) "They are those who deny the Ayât (proofs, evidences, verses, lessons, signs, revelations, etc.) of their Lord and the Meeting with Him (in the Hereafter). So their works are in vain, and on the Day of Resurrection, We shall assign not weight for them. (105) "That shall be their recompense, Hell; because they disbelieved and took My Ayât (proofs, evidences, verses, lessons, signs, revelations, etc.) and My Messengers by way of jest and mockery.

Quran 19:35-39

It befits not (the Majesty of) Allâh that He should beget a son [this refers to the slander of Christians against Allâh, by saying that 'Īsā (Jesus) is the son of Allâh]. Glorified (and Exalted is He above all that they associate with Him). When He decrees a thing, He only says to it, "Be!" and it is (35) ['Īsā (Jesus) said]: "And verily Allâh is my Lord and your Lord. So worship Him (Alone). That is the Straight Path. (Allâh's religion of Islâmic Monotheism which He did ordain for all of His Prophets)." (36) Then the sects differed [i.e. the Christians about 'Īsā (Jesus)], so woe unto the disbelievers [those who gave false witness by saying that 'Īsā (Jesus) is the son of Allâh] from the Meeting of a great Day (i.e. the Day of Resurrection, when they will be thrown in the blazing Fire). (37) How clearly will they (polytheists and disbelievers in the Oneness of Allâh) see and hear, the Day when they will appear before Us!

But the Zalimûn (polytheists and wrong-doers) today are in plain error (38) And warn them of the Day of grief and regrets, when the case has been decided, while (now) they are in a state of carelessness, and they believe not

Quran 19:54

And mention in the Book Ismâ'il (Ishmael). Verily! he was true to what he promised, and he was a Messenger, (and) a Prophet.

Quran 19:59

Then, there has succeeded them a posterity who have given up As-Salât (the prayers) [i.e. made their Salât (prayers) to be lost, either by not offering them or by not offering them perfectly or by not offering them in their proper fixed times] and have followed lusts. So they will be thrown in Hell.

Quran 19:73

And when Our Clear Verses are recited to them, those who disbelieve say to those who believe: "Which of the two groups (i.e. believers or disbelievers) is best in (point of) position and as regards station (place of council for consultation)."

Quran 19:88-93

And they say: "The Most Gracious (Allâh) has begotten a son (or offspring or children) [as the Jews say: 'Uzair (Ezra) is the son of Allâh, and the Christians say that He has begotten a son ['Īsā (Jesus)], and the pagan Arabs say that He has begotten daughters (angels, etc.)]." (88) Indeed you have brought forth (said) a terrible evil thing. (89) Whereby the heavens are almost torn, and the earth is split asunder, and the mountains fall in ruins, (90) That they ascribe a son (or offspring or children) to the Most Gracious (Allâh). (91) But it is not suitable for (the Majesty of) the Most

Gracious (Allâh) that He should beget a son (or offspring or children). (92) There is none in the heavens and the earth but comes unto the Most Gracious (Allâh) as a slave.

Quran 21:26-30

And they say: "The Most Gracious (Allâh) has begotten a son (or children)." Glory to Him! They [whom they call children of Allâh i.e. the angels, 'Īsā (Jesus) son of Maryam (Mary), 'Uzair (Ezra)], are but honoured slaves. (26) They speak not until He has spoken, and they act on His Command. (27) He knows what is before them, and what is behind them, and they cannot intercede except for him with whom He is pleased. And they stand in awe for fear of Him. (28) And if any of them should say: "Verily, I am an ilâh (a god) besides Him (Allâh)," such a one We should recompense with Hell. Thus We recompense the Zâlimûn (polytheists and wrong-doers). (29) Have not those who disbelieve known that the heavens and the earth were joined together as one united piece, then We parted them? And We have made from water every living thing. Will they not then believe?

Quran 21:36

And when those who disbelieved (in the Oneness of Allâh) see you (O Muhammad), they take you not except for mockery (saying): "Is this the one who talks (badly) about your gods?" While they disbelieve at the mention of the Most Gracious (Allâh).

Quran 22:17

Verily, those who believe (in Allâh and in His Messenger Muhammad), and those who are Jews, and the Sabians, and the Christians, and the Majus, and those who worship others besides Allâh, truly, Allâh will judge between them on the Day of Resurrection. Verily! Allâh is Witness over all things a witness.

Quran 22:52-57

*Never did We send a Messenger or a Prophet before you, but; when
he did recite the revelation or narrated or spoke, Shaitân (Satan)
threw (some falsehood) in it. But Allâh abolishes that which
Shaitân (Satan) throws in. Then Allâh establishes His Revelations.
And Allâh is All-Knower, All-Wise: (52) That He (Allâh) may
make what is thrown in by Shaitân (Satan) a trial for those in
whose hearts is a disease (of hypocrisy and disbelief) and whose
hearts are hardened. And certainly, the Zalimûn (polytheists and
wrong-doers) are in an opposition far-off (from the truth against
Allâh's Messenger and the believers). (53) And that those who
have been given knowledge may know that it (this Qur'ân) is the
truth from your Lord, so that they may believe therein, and their
hearts may submit to it with humility. And verily, Allâh is the
Guide of those who believe, to the Straight Path. (54) And those
who disbelieved will not cease to be in doubt about it (this Qur'ân)
until the Hour comes suddenly upon them, or there comes to them
the torment of the Day after which there will be no night (i.e. the
Day of Resurrection). (55) The sovereignty on that Day will be
that of Allâh (the one Who has no partners). He will judge between
them. So those who believed (in the Oneness of Allâh Islâmic
Monotheism) and did righteous good deeds will be in Gardens of
delight (Paradise). (56) And those who disbelieved and belied Our
Verses (of Qur'ân), for them will be a humiliating torment (in
Hell).*

Quran 22:71-74

*And they worship besides Allâh others for which He has sent down
no authority, and of which they have no knowledge and for the
Zâlimûn (wrong-doers, polytheists and disbelievers in the Oneness
of Allâh) there is no helper. (71) And when Our Clear Verses are*

recited to them, you will notice a denial on the faces of the disbelievers! They are nearly ready to attack with violence those who recite Our Verses to them. Say: "Shall I tell you of something worse than that? The Fire (of Hell) which Allâh has promised to those who disbelieved, and worst indeed is that destination!" (72) O mankind! A similitude has been coined, so listen to it (carefully): Verily! those on whom you call besides Allâh, cannot create (even) a fly, even though they combine together for the purpose. And if the fly snatches away a thing from them, they will have no power to release it from the fly. So weak are (both) the seeker and the sought. (73) They have not estimated Allâh His Rightful Estimate; Verily, Allâh is All-Strong, All-Mighty.

Quran 22:78

And strive hard in Allâh's Cause as you ought to strive (with sincerity and with all your efforts that His Name should be superior). He has chosen you (to convey His Message of Islâmic Monotheism to mankind by inviting them to His religion, of Islâm), and has not laid upon you in religion any hardship, it is the religion of your father Ibrahim (Abraham) (Islâmic Monotheism). It is He (Allâh) Who has named you Muslims both before and in this (the Qur'ân), that the Messenger (Muhammad) may be a witness over you and you be witness over mankind! So perform As¬Salât, give Zakât and hold fast to Allâh [i.e. have confidence in Allâh, and depend upon Him in all your affairs] He is your Maula (Patron, Lord), what an Excellent Maula (Patron, Lord) and what an Excellent Helper!

Quran 23:91-92

No son (or offspring or children) did Allâh beget, nor is there any ilâh (god) along with Him; (if there had been many gods), then, each god would have taken away what he had created, and some *would have tried to overcome others! Glorified is Allâh above all that they attribute to Him! (91)All-Knower of the unseen and the seen! Exalted is He over all that they associate as partners to Him!*

Quran 23:103-110

And those whose scales (of good deeds) are light, they are those who lose their ownselves, in Hell will they abide. (103) The Fire will burn their faces, and therein they will grin, with displaced lips (disfigured). (104) "Were not My Verses (this Qur'ân) recited to you, and then you used to deny them?" (105) They will say: "Our Lord! Our wretchedness overcame us, and we were (an) erring people. (106) "Our Lord! Bring us out of this; if ever we return (to evil), then indeed we shall be Zâlimûn: (polytheists, oppressors, unjust, and wrong-doers)." (107) He (Allâh) will say: "Remain you in it with ignominy! And speak you not to Me!" (108) Verily! there was a party of My slaves, who used to say: "Our Lord! We believe, so forgive us, and have mercy on us, for You are the Best of all who show mercy!" (109) But you took them for a laughingstock, so much so that they made you forget My Remembrance while you used to laugh at them!

Quran 23:117

And whoever invokes (or worships), besides Allâh, any other ilâh (god), of whom he has no proof, then his reckoning is only with his Lord. Surely! Al-Kâfirûn (the disbelievers in Allâh and in the Oneness of Allâh, polytheists, pagans, idolaters) will not be successful

Quran 24:62

The true believers are only those, who believe in (the Oneness of) Allâh and His Messenger (Muhammad), and when they are with him on some common matter, they go not away until they have asked his permission. Verily! those who ask your permission, those are they who (really) believe in Allâh and His Messenger. So if they ask your permission for some affairs of theirs, give permission to whom you will of them, and ask Allâh for their forgiveness. Truly, Allâh is Oft-Forgiving, Most Merciful.

Quran 25:2-6

He to Whom belongs the dominion of the heavens and the earth, and Who has begotten no son (children or offspring) and for Whom there is no partner in the dominion. He has created everything, and has measured it exactly according to its due measurements (2) Yet they have taken besides Him other âlihâh (gods) that created nothing but are themselves created, and possess neither hurt nor benefit for themselves, and possess no power (of causing) death, nor (of giving) life, nor of raising the dead. (3) Those who disbelieve say: "This (the Qurân) is nothing but a lie that he (Muhammad) has invented, and others have helped him at it, in fact they have produced an unjust wrong (thing) and a lie." (4) And they say: "Tales of the ancients, which he has written down, and they are dictated to him morning and afternoon." (5) Say: "It (this Qur'ân) has been sent down by Him (Allâh) (the Real Lord of the heavens and earth) Who knows the secret of the heavens and the earth. Truly, He is Oft-Forgiving, Most Merciful."

Quran 25:17-19

And on the Day when He will gather them together and that which they worship besides Allâh [idols, angels, pious men, saints, 'Īsā (Jesus) son of Maryam (Mary), etc.]. He will say: "Was it you who misled these My slaves or did they (themselves) stray from the (Right) Path?" (17) They will say: "Glorified are You! It was not for us to take any Auliyâ' (Protectors, Helpers) besides You, but You gave them and their fathers comfort till they forgot the

warning, and became a lost people (doomed to total loss). (18)
Thus they (false gods – all deities other than Allâh) will belie you
(polytheists) regarding what you say (that they are gods besides
Allâh), then you can neither avert (the punishment), nor get help.
And whoever among you does wrong (i.e. sets up rivals to Allâh),
We shall make him taste a great torment.

Quran 25:55

And they (disbelievers, polytheists) worship besides Allâh, that
which can neither profit them nor harm them, and the disbeliever
is ever a helper (of the Satan) against his Lord.

Quran 26:192-202

And truly, this (the Qur'ân) is a revelation from the Lord of the
'Alamîn (mankind, jinn and all that exists), (192) Which the
trustworthy Rûh [Jibril (Gabriel)] has brought down; (193) Upon
your heart (O Muhammad) that you may be (one) of the warners,
(194) In the plain Arabic language. (195) And verily, it (the
Qur'ân, and its revelation to Prophet Muhammad) is (announced)
in the Scriptures [i.e. the Taurât (Torah) and the Injeel] of former
people. (196) Is it not a sign to them that the learned scholars (like
'Abdullâh bin Salâm who embraced Islâm) of the Children of Israel
knew it (as true)? (197) And if We had revealed it (this Qur'ân)
unto any of the non-Arabs, (198) And he had recited it unto them,
they would not have believed in it. (199) Thus have We caused it
(the denial of the Qur'ân) to enter the hearts of the Mûjrimûn
(criminals, polytheists, sinners). (200) They will not believe in it
until they see the painful torment, (201) It shall come to them of a
sudden, while they perceive it not.

Quran 28:74-75

And (remember) the Day when He (your Lord — Allâh) will call to them (those who worshipped others along with Allâh), and will say: "Where are My (so-called) partners, whom you used to assert?" (74) And We shall take out from every nation a witness, and We shall say: "Bring your proof." Then they shall know that the truth is with Allâh (Alone), and the lies (false gods) which they invented will disappear from them.

Quran 29:12-13

And those who disbelieve say to those who believe: "Follow our way and we will verily bear your sins," never will they bear anything of their sins. Surely, they are liars. (12) And verily, they shall bear their own loads, and other loads besides their own, and verily, they shall be questioned on the Day of Resurrection about that which they used to fabricate.

Quran 29:46-52

And argue not with the people of the Scripture (Jews and Christians), unless it be in (a way) that is better (with good words and in good manner, inviting them to Islâmic Monotheism with His Verses), except with such of them as do wrong, and say (to them): "We believe in that which has been revealed to us and revealed to you; our Ilâh (God) and your Ilâh (God) is One (i.e. Allâh), and to Him we have submitted (as Muslims)." (46) And thus We have sent down the Book (i.e this Qur'an) to you (O Muhammad), and those whom We gave the Scripture [the Taurât (Torah) and the Injeel aforetime] believe therein as also do some of these (who are present with you now like 'Abdullâh bin Salâm) and none but the disbelievers reject Our Ayât [(proofs, signs, verses, lessons, etc.), and deny Our Oneness of Lordship and Our Oneness of worship and Our Oneness of Our Names and Qualities: i.e. Islâmic Monotheism] (47) Neither did you (O

Muhammad) read any book before it (this Qur'ân), nor did you write any book (whatsoever) with your right hand. In that case, indeed, the followers of falsehood might have doubted. (48) Nay, but they, the clear Ayât [i.e the description and the qualities of Prophet Muhammad written in the Taurât (Torah) and the Injeel] are preserved in the breasts of those who have been given knowledge (among the people of the Scriptures). And none but the Zâlimûn (polytheists and wrongdoers) deny Our Ayât (proofs, evidences, verses, lessons, signs, revelations, etc.). (49) And they say: "Why are not signs sent down to him from his Lord? Say: "The signs are only with Allâh, and I am only a plain warner." (50) Is it not sufficient for them that We have sent down to you the Book (the Qur'ân) which is recited to them? Verily, herein is mercy and a reminder (or an admonition) for a people who believe. (51) Say (to them O Muhammad): "Sufficient is Allâh for a witness between me and you. He knows what is in the heavens and on earth." And those who believe in Bâtil (all false deities other than Allâh), and disbelieve in Allâh and (in His Oneness), it is they who are the losers.

Quran 29:68

And who does more wrong than he who invents a lie against Allâh or denies the truth (Muhammad and his doctrine of Islâmic Monotheism and this Qur'ân), when it comes to him? Is there not a dwelling in Hell for disbelievers (in the Oneness of Allâh and in His Messenger Muhammad)?

Quran 30:12-13

And on the Day when the Hour will be established, the Mujrimûn (disbelievers, sinners, criminals, polytheists) will be plunged into destruction with (deep regrets, sorrows, and) despair. (12) No intercessors will they have from those whom they made equal with

Allâh (partners i.e. their so¬called associate gods), and they will (themselves) reject and deny their partners.

Quran 30:16

And as for those who disbelieved and belied Our Ayât (proofs, evidences, verses, lessons, signs, revelations, Allâh's Messengers, Resurrection, etc.), and the Meeting of the Hereafter, such shall be brought forth to the torment (in the Hell-fire).

Quran 31:13

And (remember) when Luqmân said to his son when he was advising him: "O my son! Join not in worship others with Allâh. Verily! Joining others in worship with Allâh is a great Zûlm (wrong) indeed.

Quran 31:21

And when it is said to them: "Follow that which Allâh has sent down", they say: "Nay, we shall follow that which we found our fathers (following)." (Would they do so) even if Shaitân (Satan) invites them to the torment of the Fire?

Quran 33:65-69

Verily, Allâh has cursed the disbelievers, and has prepared for them a flaming Fire (Hell). (64) Wherein they will abide for ever, and they will find neither a Walî (a protector) nor a helper. (65) On the Day when their faces will be turned over in the Fire, they will say: "Oh, would that we had obeyed Allâh and obeyed the Messenger (Muhammad)." (66) And they will say: "Our Lord! Verily, we obeyed our chiefs and our great ones, and they misled us from the (Right) Way. (67) Our Lord! Give them double torment and curse them with a mighty curse!" (68) O you who believe! Be not like those who annoyed Mûsa (Moses), but Allâh cleared him of that which they alleged, and he was honourable before Allâh

Quran 34:22-28

Say: "Call upon those whom you assert (to be associate gods) besides Allâh, they possess not even an atom's (or a small ant's) weight either in the heavens or on the earth, nor have they any share in either, nor there is for Him any supporter from among them. (22) Intercession with Him profits not, except for him whom He permits. So much so that when fear is banished from their (angels') hearts, they (angels) say: "What is it that your Lord has said?" They say: "The truth. And He is the Most High, the Most Great." (23) Say "Who gives you provision from the heavens and the earth?" Say: "Allâh, And verily, (either) we or you are rightly guided or in plain error." (24) Say (O Muhammad) "You will not be asked about our sins, nor shall we be asked of what you do." (25) Say: "Our Lord will assemble us all together (on the Day of Resurrection), then He will judge between us with truth. And He is the Just judge, the All-Knower of the true state of affairs." (26) Say: "Show me those whom you have joined with Him as partners. Nay (there are not at all any partners with Him)! But He is Allâh (Alone), the All¬Mighty, the All¬Wise." (27) And We have not sent you (O Muhammad) except as a giver of glad tidings and a warner to all mankind, but most of men know not

Quran 34:31-33

And those who disbelieve say: "We believe not in this Qur'ân nor in that which was before it," but if you could see when the Zâlimûn (polytheists and wrong¬doers) will be made to stand before their Lord, how they will cast the (blaming) word one to another! Those who were deemed weak will say to those who were arrogant: "Had it not been for you, we should certainly have been believers!" (31) And those who were arrogant will say to those who were deemed weak: "Did we keep you back from guidance after it had come to you? Nay, but you were Mujrimûn (polytheists, sinners, disbeliveres, criminals). (32) Those who were deemed weak will say to those who were arrogant: "Nay, but it was your plotting by night and day, when you ordered us to disbelieve in Allâh and set up rivals to Him!" And each of them (parties) will conceal their own regrets (for disobeying Allâh during this worldly life), when they behold the torment. And We shall put iron collars round the necks of those who disbelieved. Are they requited aught except what they used to do?

Quran 35:18

And no bearer of burdens shall bear another's burden, and if one heavily laden calls another to (bear) his load, nothing of it will be lifted even though he be near of kin. You can warn only those who fear their Lord unseen, and perform As-Salât. And he who purifies himself (from all kinds of sins), then he purifies only for the benefit of his ownself. And to Allâh is the (final) Return (of all).

Quran 37:22-35

It will be said to the angels): "Assemble those who did wrong, together with their companions and what they used to worship (22) "Instead of Allâh, and lead them on to the way of flaming Fire (Hell); (23) "But stop them, verily they are to be questioned. (24) "What is the matter with you? Why do you not help one another (as you used to do in the world)?" (25) Nay, but that Day they shall surrender, (26) And they will turn to one another and question one another. (27) They will say: "It was you who used to come to us from the right side [i.e. from the right side of one of us and beautify for us every evil, enjoin on us polytheism, and stop us from the truth i.e. Islâmic Monotheism and from every good

*deed]." (28) They will reply: "Nay, you yourselves were not
believers. (29) "And we had no authority over you. Nay! But you
were Taghun (transgressing) people (polytheists, and disbelievers).
(30) "So now the Word of our Lord has been justified against us,
that we shall certainly (have to) taste (the torment). (31) "So we
led you astray because we were ourselves astray." (32) Then verily,
that Day, they will (all) share in the torment. (33) Certainly, that
is how We deal with Al¬Mujrimûn (polytheists, sinners,
disbelivers, criminals, the disobedient to Allâh). (34) Truly, when
it was said to them: Lâ ilâha illallâh "(none has the right to be
worshipped but Allâh)," they puffed themselves up with pride (i.e.
denied it).*

Quran 37:151-152

*Verily, it is of their falsehood that they say: (151) "Allâh has
begotten." And, verily, they are liars!*

Quran 39:3-4

*Surely, the religion (i.e. the worship and the obedience) is for Allâh
only. And those who take Auliyâ' (protectors, helpers, lords, gods)
besides Him (say): "We worship them only that they may bring us
near to Allâh." Verily, Allâh will judge between them concerning
that wherein they differ. Truly, Allâh guides not him who is a liar,
and a disbeliever. (3) Had Allâh willed to take a son (or offspring),
He could have chosen whom He willed out of those whom He
created. But glory is to Him! (He is above such things). He is
Allâh, the One, the Irresistible.*

Quran 39:7-8

*If you disbelieve, then verily, Allâh is not in need of you, He likes
not disbelief for His slaves. And if you are grateful (by being
believers), He is pleased therewith for you. No bearer of burdens*

shall bear the burden of another. Then to your Lord is your return, and He will inform you what you used to do. Verily, He is the All-Knower of that which is in (men's) breasts. (7) And when some hurt touches man, he cries to his Lord (Allâh Alone), turning to Him in repentance, but when He bestows a favour upon him from Himself, he forgets that for which he cried for before, and he sets up rivals to Allâh, in order to mislead others from His Path. Say: "Take pleasure in your disbelief for a while: surely, you are (one) of the dwellers of the Fire!"

Quran 39:32

Then, who does more wrong than one who utters a lie against Allâh, and denies the truth [this Qur'ân, the Prophet (Muhammad), and the Islâmic Monotheism] when it comes to him! Is there not in Hell an abode for the disbelievers?

Quran 39:38

And verily, if you ask them: "Who created the heavens and the earth?" Surely, they will say: "Allâh (has created them)." Say: "Tell me then, the things that you invoke besides Allâh, if Allâh intended some harm for me, could they remove His harm, or if He (Allâh) intended some mercy for me, could they withhold His Mercy?" Say : "Sufficient for me is Allâh; in Him those who trust (i.e. believers) must put their trust."

Quran 39:43-45

Have they taken (others) as intercessors besides Allâh? Say: "Even if they have power over nothing whatever and have no intelligence?" (43) Say: "To Allâh belongs all intercession. His is the Sovereignty of the heavens and the earth, Then to Him you shall be brought back." (44) And when Allâh Alone is mentioned, the hearts of those who believe not in the Hereafter are filled with *disgust (from the Oneness of Allâh) and when those (whom they obey or worship) besides Him [like all false deities other than Allâh, it may be a Messenger, an angel, a pious man, a jinn, or any other creature even idols, graves of religious people, saints, priests, monks and others] are mentioned, behold, they rejoice!*

Quran 39:64-67

Say: "Do you order me to worship other than Allâh? O you fools!" (64) And indeed it has been revealed to you (O Muhammad), as it was to those (Allâh's Messengers) before you: "If you join others in worship with Allâh, (then) surely (all) your deeds will be in vain, and you will certainly be among the losers." (65) Nay! But worship Allâh (Alone and none else), and be among the grateful. (66) They made not a just estimate of Allâh such as is due to Him. And on the Day of Resurrection the whole of the earth will be grasped by His Hand and the heavens will be rolled up in His Right Hand. Glorified is He, and High is He above all that they associate as partners with Him!

Quran 40:4

None disputes in the Ayât (proofs, evidences, verses, lessons, signs, revelations, etc.) of Allâh but those who disbelieve. So let not their ability of going about here and there through the land (for their purposes) deceive you [O Muhammad, for their ultimate end will be the Fire of Hell]!

Quran 40:12

(It will be said when disbelievers are in hell): "This is because, when Allâh Alone was invoked (in worship) you disbelieved, but when partners were joined to Him, you believed (denied)! So the judgement is only with Allâh, the Most High, the Most Great!"

Quran 40:60

And your Lord said: "Invoke Me, [i.e. believe in My Oneness (Islâmic Monotheism)] (and ask Me for anything) I will respond to your (invocation). Verily! Those who scorn My worship [i.e. do not invoke Me, and do not believe in My Oneness, (Islâmic Monotheism)] they will surely enter Hell in humiliation!"

Quran 40:70-74

Those who deny the Book (this Qur'ân), and that with which We sent Our Messengers (i.e. to worship none but Allâh Alone sincerely, and to reject all false deities and to confess resurrection after the death for recompense) they will come to know (when they will be cast into the Fire of Hell). (70) When iron collars will be rounded over their necks, and the chains, they shall be dragged along (71) In the boiling water, then they will be burned in the Fire. (72) Then it will be said to them: "Where are (all) those whom you used to join in worship as partners. (73) Besides Allâh?" They will say: "They have vanished from us: Nay, we did not invoke (worship) anything before." Thus Allâh leads astray the disbelievers.

Quran 41:26

And those who disbelieve say: "Listen not to this Qur'ân, and make noise in the midst of its (recitation) that you may overcome."

Quran 41:52

Say: "Tell me, if it (the Qur'ân) is from Allâh, and you disbelieve in it, who is more astray than one who is in opposition far away (from Allâh's Right Path and His obedience).

Quran 43:63-65

And when 'Īsā (Jesus) came with (Our) clear Proofs, he said: "I have come to you with Al-Hikmah (Prophethood), and in order to make clear to you some of the (points) in which you differ, Therefore fear Allâh and obey me, (63) "Verily, Allâh! He is my Lord (God) and your Lord (God). So worship Him (Alone). This is the (only) Straight Path (i.e. Allâh's religion of true Islâmic Monotheism)." (64) But the sects from among themselves differed. So woe to those who do wrong (by ascribing things to 'Īsā (Jesus) that are not true) from the torment of a painful Day (i.e. the Day of Resurrection)!

Quran 43:81-83

Say (O Muhammad): "If the Most Gracious (Allâh) had a son (or children as you pretend), then I am the first of Allâh's worshippers [who deny and refute this claim of yours (and the first to believe in Allâh Alone and testify that He has no children)]." (81) Glorified is the Lord of the heavens and the earth, the Lord of the Throne! Exalted is He from all that they ascribe (to Him). (82) So leave them (alone) to speak nonsense and play until they meet the Day of theirs, which they have been promised.

Quran 45:7-11

Woe to every sinful liar, (7) Who hears the Verses of Allâh (being) recited to him, yet persists with pride as if he heard them not. So announce to him a painful torment! (8) And when he learns something of Our Verses (this Qur'ân), he makes them a jest. For such there will be a humiliating torment. (9) In front of them there is Hell, and that which they have earned will be of no profit to them, nor (will be of any profit to them) those whom they have taken as Auliyâ' (protectors, helpers) besides Allâh. And theirs will be a great torment. (10) This (Qur'ân) is a guidance. And those who disbelieve in the Ayât (proofs, evidences, verses, lessons, signs, revelations) of their Lord, for them there is a painful torment of Rijz (a severe kind of punishment).

Quran 46:7-12

And when Our Clear Verses are recited to them, the disbelievers say of the truth (this Qur'ân), when it reaches them: "This is plain magic!" (7) Or say they: "He (Muhammad) has fabricated it." Say: "If I have fabricated it still you have no power to support me against Allâh. He knows best of what you say among yourselves concerning it (i.e. this Qur'ân)! Sufficient is He as a witness between me and you! And He is the Oft-Forgiving, the Most Merciful." (8) Say (O Muhammad):"I am not a new thing among the Messengers (of Allâh) (i.e. I am not the first Messenger) nor do I know what will be done with me or with you. I only follow that which is revealed to me, and I am but a plain warner." (9) Say: "Tell me! If this (Qur'ân) is from Allâh and you deny it, and a witness from among the Children of Israel ('Abdullâh bin Salâm) testifies that [this Qur'ân is from Allâh (like the Taurât (Torah)], and he believed (embraced Islâm) while you are too proud (to believe)." Verily, Allâh guides not the people who are Zâlimûn (polytheists, disbelievers and wrong-doers). (10) And those who disbelieve (strong and wealthy) say of those who believe (the weak and poor): "Had it (Islâmic Monotheism to which Muhammad is inviting mankind) been a good thing, they (the weak and poor) would not have preceded us thereto!" And when they have not let themselves be guided by it (this Qur'ân), they say: "This is an ancient lie!" (11) And before this was the Scripture of Mûsâ (Moses) as a guide and a mercy. And this is a confirming Book (the Qur'ân) in the Arabic language, to warn those who do wrong, and as glad tidings to the Muhsinûn (good-doers).

Quran 47:8-9

But those who disbelieve (in the Oneness of Allâh Islâmic Monotheism), for them is destruction, and (Allâh) will make their deeds vain. (8) That is because they hate that which Allâh has sent down (this Qur'ân and Islâmic laws etc.), so He has made their deeds fruitless.

Quran 48:6

And that He may punish the Munâfiqûn (hypocrites), men and women, and also the Mushrikûn men and women, who think evil thoughts about Allâh, for them is a disgraceful torment, And the Anger of Allâh is upon them, and He has cursed them and prepared Hell for them — and worst indeed is that destination.

Quran 49:15

Only those are the believers who have believed in Allâh and His Messenger, and afterward doubt not but strive with their wealth and their lives for the Cause of Allâh. Those! They are the truthful.

Quran 57:16

Has not the time come for the hearts of those who believe (in the Oneness of Allâh - Islâmic Monotheism) to be affected by Allâh's Reminder (this Qur'ân), and that which has been revealed of the truth, lest they become as those who received the Scripture [the Taurât (Torah) and the Injeel] before (i.e. Jews and Christians), and the term was prolonged for them and so their hearts were hardened? And many of them were Fâsiqûn (the rebellious, the disobedient to Allâh).

Quran 57:26-29

And indeed, We sent Nûh (Noah) and Ibrahîm (Abraham), and placed in their offspring Prophethood and Scripture, And among them there are some who are guided, but many of them are Fâsiqûn (rebellious, disobedient to Allâh). (26) Then, We sent after them, Our Messengers, and We sent 'Îsâ (Jesus) son of Maryam (Mary), and gave him the Injeel. And We ordained in the hearts of those who followed him, compassion and mercy. But the monasticism which they invented for themselves, We did not prescribe for them, but (they sought it) only to please Allâh therewith, but they did not observe it with the right observance. So We gave those among them who believed, their (due) reward, but many of them are Fâsiqûn (rebellious, disobedient to Allâh). (27) O you who believe [in Mûsa (Moses) (i.e. Jews) and 'Îsâ (Jesus) (i.e. Christians)]! Fear Allâh, and believe in His Messenger (Muhammad), He will give you a double portion of His Mercy, and He will give you a light by which you shall walk (straight), and He will forgive you. And Allâh is Oft-Forgiving, Most Merciful. (28) So that the people of the Scripture (Jews and Christians) may know that they have no power whatsoever over the Grace of Allâh, and that (His) Grace is (entirely) in His Hand to bestow it on whomsoever He wills. And Allâh is the Owner of Great Bounty.

Quran 58:8

Have you not seen those who were forbidden to hold secret counsels, and afterwards returned to that which they had been forbidden, and conspired together for sin and wrong doing and disobedience to the Messenger (Muhammad). And when they come to you, they greet you with a greeting wherewith Allâh greets you not, and say within themselves: "Why should Allâh punish us not for what we say?" Hell will be sufficient for them, they will burn therein, and worst indeed is that destination!

Muqatil bin Hayyan, said, "The Prophet had a peace treaty with the Jews. When one of the Prophet's Companions would pass by a gathering of Jews, they would speak among themselves in secret, prompting the believer to think that they were plotting to kill or harm him. When the believer saw this, he feared for his safety and changed the route he was taking. The Prophet advised them to abandon their evil secret talks, but they did not listen and kept on holding the Najwa."

Quran 58:14-15

Have you (O Muhammad) not seen those (hypocrites) who take as friends a people upon whom is the Wrath of Allâh (i.e. Jews)? They are neither of you (Muslims) nor of them (Jews), and they swear to a lie while they know. (14) Allâh has prepared for them a severe torment. Evil indeed is that which they used to do.

Quran 58:22

You will not find any people who believe in Allâh and the Last Day, making friendship with those who oppose Allâh and His Messenger (Muhammad), even though they were their fathers or their sons or their brothers or their kindred (people). For such He has written Faith in their hearts, and strengthened them with Rûh (proofs, light and true guidance) from Himself. And He will admit them to Gardens (Paradise) under which rivers flow to dwell therein (forever). Allâh is pleased with them, and they with Him. They are the Party of Allâh. Verily, it is the Party of Allâh that will be the successful.

Quran 59:11

Have you (O Muhammad) not observed the hypocrites who say to their friends among the people of the Scripture who disbelieve: "(By Allâh) If you are expelled, we (too) indeed will go out with you, and we shall never obey any one against you, and if you are attacked (in fight), we shall indeed help you." But Allâh is Witness, that they verily, are liars.

Quran 60:13

O you who believe! Take not as friends the people who incurred the Wrath of Allâh (i.e. the Jews). Surely, they have despaired of (receiving any good in) the Hereafter, just as the disbelievers have despaired of those (buried) in graves (that they will not be resurrected on the Day of Resurrection).

Quran 61:5-9

And (remember) when Mûsa (Moses) said to his people: "O my people! Why do you annoy me while you know certainly that I am the Messenger of Allâh to you? So when they turned away (from the Path of Allâh), Allâh turned their hearts away (from the Right Path). And Allâh guides not the people who are Fâsiqûn (the rebellious, the disobedient to Allâh). (5) And (remember) when 'Īsā (Jesus), son of Maryam (Mary), said: "O Children of Israel! I am the Messenger of Allâh unto you confirming the Taurât [(Torah) which came] before me, and giving glad tidings of a Messenger to come after me, whose name shall be Ahmed . But when he (Ahmed i.e. Muhammad) came to them with clear proofs, they said: "This is plain magic." (6) And who does more wrong than the one who invents a lie against Allâh, while he is being invited to Islâm? And Allâh guides not the people who are Zâlimûn (polytheists, wrong-doers and disbelievers) folk. (7) They intend to put out the Light of Allâh (i.e. the Religion of Islâm, this Qur'ân, and the Prophet Muhammad) with their mouths. But Allâh will bring His Light to perfection even though the disbelievers hate (it). (8) He it is Who has sent His Messenger (Muhammad) with guidance and the religion of truth (Islâmic Monotheism) to make it victorious over all (other) religions even though the Mushrikûn (polytheists, pagans, idolaters, and disbelievers in the Oneness of Allâh and in His Messenger Muhammed) hate (it).

Quran 61:14

O you who believe! Be you helpers (in the Cause) of Allâh as said 'Īsā (Jesus), son of Maryam (Mary), to the Hawârîyyun (the disciples) : "Who are my helpers (in the Cause) of Allâh?" The Hawârîyyun (the disciples) said: "We are Allâh's helpers" (i.e. we will strive in His Cause!). Then a group of the Children of Israel believed and a group disbelieved. So We gave power to those who believed against their enemies, and they became the victorious (uppermost).

Quran 62:5-8

The likeness of those who were entrusted with the (obligation of the) Taurât (Torah) (i.e. to obey its commandments and to practise its laws), but who subsequently failed in those (obligations), is as the likeness of a donkey which carries huge burdens of books (but understunds nothing from them). How bad is the example of people who deny the Ayât (proofs, evidences, verses, signs, revelations) of Allâh. And Allâh guides not the people who are Zâlimûn (polytheists, wrong-doers, disbelievers). (5) Say: "O you Jews! If you pretend that you are friends of Allâh, to the exclusion of (all) other mankind, then long for death if you are truthful." (6) But they will never long for it (death), because of what (deeds) their hands have sent before them! And Allâh knows well the Zâlimûn (polytheists, wrong-doers, disbelievers). (7) Say (to them): "Verily, the death from which you flee will surely meet you, then you will be sent back to (Allâh), the All-Knower of the unseen and the seen, and He will tell you what you used to do."

Quran 64:14

O you who believe! Verily, among your wives and your children are your enemies (who may stop you from the obedience of Allâh), therefore beware of them! But if you pardon (them) and overlook, and forgive (their faults), then verily, Allâh is Oft-Forgiving, Most Merciful.

Allah states that some wives and children are enemies to their husbands and fathers, in that they might be busied with them rather than with performing the good deeds. Specifically, this ayah was revealed in relation to men who embraced Islam in Makkah and wanted to migrate to Allah's Messenger. However, their wives and children refused to allow them. Later when they joined Allah's Messenger, they found that those who were with him (the Companions) have gained knowledge in the religion, so they were about to punish their wives and children. Allah then sent down this Ayah, (*But if you pardon (them) and overlook, and forgive, then verily, Allah is Oft-Forgiving, Most Merciful.*)" At-Tirmidhi collected this Hadith and said that it is Hasan Sahih. If this is the case with such wives being enemies merely because of the postponement of Hijrah and knowledge seeking, then clearly Ahl-Kitab being marriable in no way disqualifies them from being enemies; especially when Christians and Jews have already been labeled disbelievers, enemies of Allah and his Messenger and allies of Shaitan. Simply being married to a Muslim man does not mean you cannot simultaneously be his enemy. The wives of Noah and Lot are examples of ahl-kitab enemies married to Muslim men.

Quran 66:12

And Maryam (Mary), the daughter of 'Imrân who guarded her chastity; and We breathed into (the sleeve of her shirt or her

[82]

garment) through Our Rûh [i.e. Jibril (Gabriel)], and she testified to the truth of the Words of her Lord [i.e. believed in the Words of Allâh: "Be!" and he was; that is 'Īsā (Jesus) son of Maryam (Mary) as a Messenger of Allâh], and (also believed in) His Scriptures, and she was of the Qanitun (i.e. obedient to Allâh)

Quran 67:6-9

And for those who disbelieve in their Lord (Allâh) is the torment of Hell, and worst indeed is that destination (6) When they are cast therein, they will hear the (terrible) drawing in of its breath as it blazes forth (7) It almost bursts up with fury. Every time a group is cast therein, its keeper will ask: "Did no warner come to you?" (8) They will say: "Yes indeed a warner did come to us, but we belied him and said: 'Allâh never sent down anything (of revelation), you are only in great error.'"

Quran 68:35

Shall We then treat the Muslims (believers of Islamic Monotheism, doers of righteous deeds) like the Mujrimûn (criminals, polytheists and disbelievers)?

Quran 74:31

And We have set none but angels as guardians of the Fire, and We have fixed number (19) only as a trial for the disbelievers, in order that the people of the Scripture (Jews and Christians) may arrive at a certainty [that this Qur'ân is the truth as it agrees with their Books regarding their number (19) which is written in the Taurât (Torah) and the Injeel] and that the believers may increase in Faith (as this Qur'ân is the truth) and that no doubt may be left for the people of the Scripture and the believers, and that those in whose hearts is a disease (of hypocrisy) and the disbelievers may say: "What Allâh intends by this (curious) example ?" Thus Allâh leads astray whom He wills and guides whom He wills. And none can know the hosts of your Lord but He. And this (Hell) is nothing else than a (warning) reminder to mankind.

Quran 74:40-48

In Gardens (Paradise) they will ask one another, (40) About Al-Mujrimûn (polytheists, criminals, disbelievers), (And they will say to them): (41) "What has caused you to enter Hell?" (42) They will say: "We were not of those who used to offer the Salât (prayers) (43) "Nor we used to feed Al-Miskin (the poor); (44) "And we used to talk falsehood (all that which Allâh hated) with vain talkers (45) "And we used to belie the Day of Recompense (46) "Until there came to us (the death) that is certain." (47) So no intercession of intercessors will be of any use to them

Quran 75:31-35

So he (the disbeliever) neither believed (in this Qur'ân, and in the Message of Muhammad) nor prayed!(Salat) (31) But on the contrary, he belied (this Qur'ân and the Message of Muhammad) and turned away! (32) Then he walked in conceit (full pride) to his family admiring himself! (33) Woe to you [O man (disbeliever)]! And then (again) woe to you! (34) Again, woe to you [O man (disbeliever)]! And then (again) woe to you!

Quran 84:20-24

What is the matter with them, that they believe not? (20) And when the Qur'ân is recited to them, they fall not prostrate, (21) Nay, those who disbelieve, belie (Prophet Muhammad and whatever he brought, i.e. this Qur'ân and Islâmic Monotheism, etc.) (22) And Allâh knows best what they gather (of good and bad deeds), (23) So announce to them a painful torment.

Quran 98:1-7

Those who disbelieve from among the people of the Scripture (Jews and Christians) and Al-Mushrikûn, were not going to leave (their disbelief) until there came to them clear evidence (1) A Messenger (Muhammad) from Allâh, reciting (the Qur'ân) purified pages [purified from Al-Bâtil (falsehood)] (2) Wherein are correct and straight laws from Allâh. (3) And the people of the Scripture (Jews and Christians) differed not until after there came to them clear evidence. (4) And they were commanded not, but that they should worship Allâh, and worship none but Him Alone (abstaining from ascribing partners to Him), and perform As-Salât and give Zakât: and that is the right religion. (5) Verily, those who disbelieve (in the religion of Islâm, the Qur'ân and Prophet Muhammad) from among the people of the Scripture (Jews and Christians) and Al-Mushrikûn will abide in the Fire of Hell. They are the worst of creatures. (6) Verily, those who believe [in the Oneness of Allâh, and in His Messenger (Muhammad) including all obligations ordered by Islâm] and do righteous good deeds, they are the best of creatures

Quran 103:1-3

By Al-'Asr (the time). (1) Verily, man is in loss, (2) Except those who believe (in Islâmic Monotheism) and do righteous good deeds, and recommend one another to the truth (i.e. order one another to perform all kinds of good deeds (Al-Ma'ruf) which Allâh has ordained, and abstain from all kinds of sins and evil deeds (Al-Munkar) which Allâh has forbidden), and recommend one another to patience (for the sufferings, harms, and injuries which one may encounter in Allâh's Cause during preaching His religion of Islâmic Monotheism or Jihâd).

Quran 109:1-6

Say: "O Al-Kâfirûn (disbelievers in Allâh, in His Oneness, in His Angels, in His Books, in His Messengers, in the Day of Resurrection, and in Al-Qadar)! (1) "I worship not that which you worship, (2) "Nor will you worship that which I worship. (3) "And I shall not worship that which you are worshipping. (4) "Nor will you worship that which I worship. (5) "To you be your religion, and to me my religion.

Though this was revealed in context of pagans the ruling lets us know the definition of a kafir/disbeliever as one who doesn't worship what Muhammad pbuh worshipped the way he did. Also if one worships other than what Muhammad pbuh worshipped then they are also a kafir/disbeliever.

Quran 112:1-4

Say: "He is Allâh, (the) One. (1) "Allâh-us-Samad [Allâh the Self-Sufficient Master, Whom all creatures need, (He neither eats nor drinks)]. (2) "He begets not, nor was He begotten; (3) "And there is none co-equal or comparable unto Him."

Abu Huraira reported Allah's Messenger (ﷺ) as saying:

If ten scholars of the Jews would follow me, no Jew would be left upon the surface of the earth who would not embrace Islam.

Source: Sahih Muslim 2793

Narrated Abu Sa`id:

The Prophet said, "You will follow the wrong ways, of your predecessors so completely and literally that if they should go into the hole of a mastigure, you too will go there." We said, "O Allah's Messenger! Do you mean the Jews and the Christians?" He replied, "Whom else?" (Meaning, of course, the Jews and the Christians.)

Source: Sahih al-Bukhari 3456

Narrated 'Amr bin Shu'aib:

from his father, from his grandfather, that the Messenger of Allah said: "He is not one of us who resembles other than us, nor who resembles the Jews nor the Christians. For indeed greeting of the Jews is pointing the finger, and the greeting of the Christians is waving with the hand."

Source: Jami` at-Tirmidhi 2695 Graded Daif by Darussalam

Narrated Abu Hurairah:

The Prophet as saying: Jews and Christians do not dye (their beards), so act differently from them.

Source: Sunan Abi Dawud 4203 Graded Sahih by Albani

Narrated Abi Aiyub:

Once the Prophet went out after sunset and heard a dreadful voice, and said, "The Jews are being punished in their graves."

Source: Sahih al-Bukhari 1375

Narrated Abu Huraira:

Allah's Messenger said, "May Allah curse the Jews, because Allah made fat illegal for them but they sold it and ate its price. "

Source: Sahih al-Bukhari 2224

Narrated Abu Huraira:

While we were in the mosque, Allah's Messenger came out to us and said, "Let us proceed to the Jews." So we went along with him till we reached Bait-al-Midras (a place where the Torah used to be recited and all the Jews of the town used to gather). The Prophet stood up and addressed them, "O Assembly of Jews! Embrace Islam and you will be safe!" The Jews replied, "O Aba-l-Qasim! You have conveyed Allah's message to us." The Prophet said, "That is what I want (from you)." He repeated his first statement for the second time, and they said, "You have conveyed Allah's message, O Aba-l- Qasim." Then he said it for the third time and added, "You should Know that the earth belongs to Allah and His Apostle, and I want to exile you from this land, so whoever among you owns some property, can sell it, otherwise you should know that the Earth belongs to Allah and His Apostle."

Source: Sahih al-Bukhari 6944

It has been narrated by 'Umar b. al-Khattib that he heard the Messenger of Allah (ﷺ) say:

I will expel the Jews and Christians from the Arabian Peninsula and will not leave any but Muslim.

Source: Sahih Muslim 1767 a

Abu Musa' reported that Allah's Messenger (ﷺ) said:

When it will be the Day of Resurrection Allah would deliver to every Muslim a Jew or a Christian and say: That is your rescue from Hell-Fire.

Source: Sahih Muslim 2767 a

Narrated Aws ibn Thabit al-Ansari:

The Messenger of Allah said: Act differently from the Jews, for they do not pray in their sandals or their shoes.

Source: Sunan Abi Dawud 652 Graded Sahih by Albani

Narrated Abu Hurayrah:

The Prophet said: Religion will continue to prevail as long as people hasten to break the fast, because the Jews and the Christians delay doing so.

Source: Sunan Abi Dawud 2353 Graded Hasan by Albani

Narrated Zaid bin Thabit:

"The Messenger of Allah ordered me to learn some statements from writings of the Jews for him, and he said: 'For indeed by Allah! I do no trust the Jews with my letters.'" He said: "Half a month did not pass before I learned it, when he wanted to write to the Jews I would write it to them, and when they wrote to him I would read their letters to him."

Source: Jami` at-Tirmidhi 2715

Graded Hasan by Darussalam

It was narrated from 'Awf bin Malik that the Messenger of Allah(ﷺ) said:

"The Jews split into seventy-one sects, one of which will be in Paradise and seventy in Hell. The Christians split into seventy-two sects, seventy-one of which will be in Hell and one in Paradise. I swear by the One Whose Hand is the soul of Muhammad, my nation will split into seventy-three sects, one of which will be in Paradise and seventy-two in Hell." It was said: "O Messenger of Allah, who are they?" He said: "The main body."

Source: Sunan Ibn Majah 3992 Graded Hasan by Darussalam

Narrated Abu Hurairah:

that the Messenger of Allah said: "Do not precede the Jews and the Christians with the Salam. And if one of you meets them in the path, then force them to its narrow portion."

Source: Jami` at-Tirmidhi 2700 Graded Sahih by Darussalam

It was narrated from 'Amr Bin Shu'aib, from his father, that his grandfather said:

"The Messenger of Allah said: 'The blood money for Ahl Adh-Dhimmah is half that of the blood money for the Muslims, and they are the Jews and Christians."

Source: Sunan an-Nasa'i 4806 Graded Hasan by Darussalam

Narrated Abu Huraira:

The people of the Scripture (Jews) used to recite the Torah in Hebrew and they used to explain it in Arabic to the Muslims. On that Allah's Messenger said, "Do not believe the people of the Scripture or disbelieve them, but say:-- "We believe in Allah and what is revealed to us."

Source: Sahih al-Bukhari 4485

Ali narrated that :

The Messenger of Allah said: "Whoever has the provisions and the means to convey him to Allah's House and he does not perform Hajj, then it does not matter if he dies as a Jew or a Christian. That is because Allah said in His Book: 'And Hajj to the House is a duty that mankind owes to Allah, for whomever is able to bear the journey.'

[90]

Source: Jami` at-Tirmidhi 812 Graded Daif by Darussalam

It was narrated from Anas that:

a funeral passed by the Messenger of Allah and he stood up. It was said: "It is the funeral of a Jew." He said: "We stood up for the angels."

Source: Sunan an-Nasa'i 1929 Graded Hasan by Darussalam

Narrated Ubadah ibn as-Samit:

The Messenger of Allah used to stand up for a funeral until the corpse was placed in the grave. A learned Jew (once) passed him and said: This is how we do. The Prophet sat down and said: Sit down and act differently from them.

Source: Sunan Abi Dawud 3176

Graded Hasan by Albani

It was narrated from Muhammad that:

a funeral passed by Al-Hasan bin 'Ali and Ibn 'Abbas. Al-Hasan stood up but Ibn 'Abbas did not/ Al-Hasan said: 'Didn't the Messenger of Allah stand up for the funeral of a Jew?' Ibn 'Abbas said: 'Yes, then he sat down."'

Source: Sunan an-Nasa'i 1924 Graded Sahih by Darussalam

Narrated Thabit bin Ad-Dahhak:

The Prophet said, "Whoever intentionally swears falsely by a religion other than Islam, then he is what he has said, (e.g. if he says, 'If such thing is not true then I am a Jew,' he is really a Jew). And whoever commits suicide with piece of iron will be punished with the same piece of iron in the Hell Fire."

Source: Sahih al-Bukhari 1363

Narrated Safwan bin Assal:

"A Jew said to his companion: 'Accompany us to this Prophet.' So his companion said: 'Do not say: "Prophet". For if he hears you (say that) then he will be very happy.' So they went to the Messenger of Allah to question him about nine clear signs. So he said to them: 'Do not associate anything with Allah, nor steal, nor commit unlawful intercourse, nor take a life which Allah has made prohibited, except for what is required (in the law), nor hasten to damage the reputation of one of power so that he will be killed, nor practice magic, nor consume Riba(interest), nor falsely accuse the chaste woman, nor turn to flee on the day of the march, and for you Jews particularly, to not violate the Sabbath.'" He said: "So they kissed his hands and his feet, and they said: 'We bear witness that you are a Prophet.' So he said: 'Then what prevents you from following me?' They said: 'Because Dawud supplicated to his Lord that his offspring never be devoid of Prophets and we feared that if we follow you then the Jews will kill us.'"

Source: Jami` at-Tirmidhi 2733

Graded Hasan by Darussalam

It is narrated on the authority of Abu Huraira that the Messenger of Allah (ﷺ) observed:

By Him in Whose hand is the life of Muhammad, he who amongst the community of Jews or Christians hears about me, but does not affirm his belief in that with which I have been sent and dies in this state (of disbelief), he shall be but one of the denizens of Hell-Fire.

Source: Sahih Muslim 153

Narrated `Aisha and Ibn `Abbas:

On his death-bed Allah's Messenger put a sheet over his-face and when he felt hot, he would remove it from his face. When in that state (of putting and removing the sheet) he said, "May Allah's Curse be on the Jews and the Christians for they build places of worship at the graves of their prophets." (By that) he intended to warn (the Muslim) from what they (i.e. Jews and Christians) had done.

Source: Sahih al-Bukhari 3453, 3454

Narrated Abu Huraira:

Allah's Messenger said, "No child is born but has the Islamic Faith, but its parents turn it into a Jew or a Christian. It is as you help the animals give birth. Do you find among their offspring a mutilated one before you mutilate them yourself?" The people said, "O Allah's Messenger! What do you think about those (of them) who die young?" The Prophet said, "Allah knows what they would have done (were they to live)."

Source: Sahih al-Bukhari 6599, 6600

Narrated Anas:

When the news of the arrival of the Prophet at Medina reached `Abdullah bin Salam, he went to him to ask him about certain things, He said, "I am going to ask you about three things which only a Prophet can answer: What is the first sign of The Hour? What is the first food which the people of Paradise will eat? Why does a child attract the similarity to his father or to his mother?" The Prophet replied, "Gabriel has just now informed me of that." Ibn Salam said, "He (i.e. Gabriel) is the enemy of the Jews amongst the angels. The Prophet said, "As for the first sign of The Hour, it will be a fire that will collect the people from the East to the West. As for the first meal which the people of Paradise will eat, it will be the caudate (extra) lobe of the fish-liver. As for the child, if the man's discharge proceeds the woman's discharge, the child attracts the similarity to the man, and if the woman's discharge proceeds the man's, then the child attracts the similarity to the woman." On this, `Abdullah bin Salam said, "I testify that None has the right to be worshipped except Allah, and that you are the Messenger of Allah." and added, "O Allah's Messenger! Jews invent such lies as make one astonished, so please ask them about me before they know about my conversion to Islam . " The Jews came, and the Prophet said, "What kind of man is `Abdullah bin Salam among you?" They replied, "The best of us and the son of the best of us and the most superior among us, and the son of the most superior among us. "The Prophet said, "What would you think if `Abdullah bin Salam should embrace Islam?" They said, "May Allah protect him from that." The Prophet repeated his question and they gave the same answer. Then `Abdullah came out to them and said, "I testify that None has the right to be worshipped except Allah and that Muhammad is the Messenger of Allah!" On this, the Jews said, "He is the most wicked among us and the son of the most wicked among us." So they degraded him. On this, he (i.e. `Abdullah bin Salam) said, "It is this that I was afraid of, O Allah's Messenger.

Source: Sahih al-Bukhari 3938

Yahya related to me from Malik from Ismail ibn Abi Hakim that he heard Umar ibn Abd al-Aziz say:

"One of the last things that the Messenger of Allah, said was, 'May Allah fight the jews and the christians. They took the graves of their Prophets as places of prostration . Two deens(religions) shall not co-exist in the land of the Arabs.'

Source: Muwatta imam Malik Book 45, Hadith 17

It was narrated from Abu Laila bin 'Abdullah bin 'Abdur-Rahman bin Sahl, from Sahl bin Abi Hathmah, that:

he informed him, and some men among the elders of his people, that "Abdullah bin Sahl and Muhayysah set out for Khaibar because of some problem that had arisen. Someone came to Muhayysah, and he told him that 'Abdullah bin Sahl had been killed and thrown into a pit or well. He came to the Jews and said: "By Allah, you killed him." They said: "By Allah, we did not kill him." Then he went baack to his people and told them about that. Then he and his brother Huwayysah, who was older than him, and 'Abdur-Rahman bin Sahl, came (to the prophet). Muhayysah, who was the one who had been at Khaibar, bnegan to speak, but the Messenger of Allah said: "Let the elder speak first." So Huwayysah spoke, then Muhayysah spoke. The Messenger of Allah said: "Either (the Jews) will pay the Diyah for your companion, or war will be declared on them." The Messenger of Allah sent a letter to that effect (to the Jews) and they wrote back saying: "By Allah, we did not kill him." The Messenger of Allah and 'Abdur-Rahman: "Will you swear an oath establishing your claim to the blood money of your companion?" They said: "No." He said: "Should the Jews swear an oath for you?" They said: "They are not Muslims." So the Messenger of Allah paid it himself, and he sent one hundred she-camels to their abodes. Sahl said: "A red she-camel from among them kicked me."

Source: Sunan an-Nasa'i 4711 Graded Sahih by Darussalam

Narrated Rafi` bin Khadij and Sahl bin Abu Hathma:

`Abdullah bin Sahl and Muhaiyisa bin Mas`ud went to Khaibar and they dispersed in the gardens of the date-palm trees. `Abdullah bin Sahl was murdered. Then `Abdur-Rahman bin Sahl, Huwaiyisa and Muhaiyisa, the two sons of Mas`ud, came to the

Prophet and spoke about the case of their (murdered) friend.
`Abdur-Rahman who was the youngest of them all, started talking.
The Prophet said, "Let the older (among you) speak first." So they
spoke about the case of their (murdered) friend. The Prophet said,
"Will fifty of you take an oath whereby you will have the right to
receive the blood money of your murdered man," (or said, "..your
companion"). They said, "O Allah's Messenger! The murder was a
thing we did not witness." The Prophet said, "Then the Jews will
release you from the oath, if fifty of them (the Jews) should take an
oath to contradict your claim." They said, "O Allah's Messenger !
They are disbelievers (and they will take a false oath)." Then
Allah's Messenger himself paid the blood money to them.

Source: Sahih al-Bukhari 6142, 6143

Narrated Abu Musa:

The Prophet said, "The example of Muslims, Jews and Christians
is like the example of a man who employed laborers to work for him
from morning till night. They worked till midday and they said,
'We are not in need of your reward.' So the man employed another
batch and said to them, 'Complete the rest of the day and yours
will be the wages I had fixed (for the first batch). They worked until
the time of the `Asr prayer and said, 'Whatever we have done is for
you.' He employed another batch. They worked for the rest of the
day till sunset, and they received the wages of the two former
batches."

Source: Sahih al-Bukhari 558

It was narrated that 'Ali said:

The Prophet said to me: "You are like 'Eesa(Jesus) (in some way);
the Jews hated him so much that they made false accusations
against his mother, and the Christians loved him so much that they

raised him to a status that is not appropriate for him." Then he said: Two types of men will be doomed because of me: one who loves me and goes to extremes and praises me for that which I do not have, and one who hates me and his hatred of me makes him tell lies against me.

Source: Musnad Ahmad 1376 Graded Daif by Darussalam

Narrated Abu Huraira:

When Khaibar was conquered, a roasted poisoned sheep was presented to the Prophet as a gift (by the Jews). The Prophet ordered, "Let all the Jews who have been here, be assembled before me." The Jews were collected and the Prophet said (to them), "I am going to ask you a question. Will you tell the truth?" They said, "Yes." The Prophet asked, "Who is your father?" They replied, "So-and-so." He said, "You have told a lie; your father is so-and-so." They said, "You are right." He said, "Will you now tell me the truth, if I ask you about something?" They replied, "Yes, O Abu Al-Qasim; and if we should tell a lie, you can realize our lie as you have done regarding our father." On that he asked, "Who are the people of the (Hell) Fire?" They said, "We shall remain in the (Hell) Fire for a short period, and after that you will replace us." The Prophet said, "You may be cursed and humiliated in it! By Allah, we shall never replace you in it." Then he asked, "Will you now tell me the truth if I ask you a question?" They said, "Yes, O Abu Al-Qasim." He asked, "Have you poisoned this sheep?" They said, "Yes." He asked, "What made you do so?" They said, "We wanted to know if you were a liar in which case we would get rid of you, and if you are a prophet then the poison would not harm you."

Source: Sahih al-Bukhari 3169

Narrated Ibn 'Umar:

Zaid bin 'Amr bin Nufail went to Sham, inquiring about a true religion to follow. He met a Jewish religious scholar and asked him about their religion. He said, "I intend to embrace your religion, so tell me something about it." The Jew said, "You will not embrace our religion unless you receive your share of Allah's Anger." Zaid said, "'I do not run except from Allah's Anger, and I will never bear a bit of it if I have the power to avoid it. Can you tell me of some other religion?" He said, "I do not know any other religion except the Hanif." Zaid enquired, "What is Hanif?" He said, "Hanif is the religion of (the prophet) Abraham who was neither a Jew nor a Christian, and he used to worship None but Allah (Alone)" Then Zaid went out and met a Christian religious scholar and told him the same as before. The Christian said, "You will not embrace our religion unless you get a share of Allah's Curse." Zaid replied, "I do not run except from Allah's Curse, and I will never bear any of Allah's Curse and His Anger if I have the power to avoid them. Will you tell me of some other religion?" He replied, "I do not know any other religion except Hanif." Zaid enquired, "What is Hanif?" He replied, Hanif is the religion of (the prophet) Abraham who was neither a Jew nor a Christian and he used to worship None but Allah (Alone)" When Zaid heard their Statement about (the religion of) Abraham, he left that place, and when he came out, he raised both his hands and said, "O Allah! I make You my Witness that I am on the religion of Abraham."

Source: Sahih al-Bukhari 3827

Narrated Abu Huraira:

Allah's Messenger said, "By Him in Whose Hands my soul is, surely (Jesus,) the son of Mary will soon descend amongst you and will judge mankind justly (as a Just Ruler); he will break the Cross and kill the pigs and there will be no Jizya (i.e. taxation taken from non Muslims). Money will be in abundance so that nobody will accept it, and a single prostration to Allah (in prayer) will be better than the whole world and whatever is in it." Abu Huraira added "If you wish, you can recite (this verse of the Book): -- 'And there is none Of the people of the Scriptures (Jews and Christians) But must believe in him (i.e Jesus as an Apostle of Allah and a human being) Before his death. And on the Day of Judgment He will be a witness Against them."

Source: Sahih al-Bukhari 3448

Narrated Abu Tha'labah Al-Khushani:

"I said: 'O Messenger of Allah! We are a people who hunt.' He said: 'If you send your dog and you mentioned the Name of Allah upon it, and he catches something for you, then eat it.' I said: 'Even if he kills it?' He said: 'Even if he kills it.' I said: 'We are a people who shoot (at game).' He said: 'What you catch with your bow, then eat it.'" He said: "Then I said:'Indeed we are a people who travel. We come across Jews, Christians, and Zoroastrians, and we do not find vessels other than theirs.' He said: 'If you do not find other than them, then wash them with water, then eat and drink from it.'"

Source: Jami` at-Tirmidhi 1464 Graded Sahih by Darussalam

Mu'adh reported:

The Messenger of Allah sent me as a governor to Yemen and (at the time of departure) he instructed me thus: "You will go to people of the Scripture (i.e., the Jews and the Christians). First of all invite them to testify that La ilaha ill Allah (There is no true god except Allah) and that Muhammad is His slave and Messenger; and if they accept this, then tell them that Allah has enjoined upon them five Salat (prayers) during the day and night; and if they accept it, then tell them that Allah has made the payment of Zakat obligatory upon them. It should be collected from their rich and distributed among their poor; and if they agree to it, don't take (as a share of Zakat) the best of their properties. Beware of the supplications of the oppressed, for there is no barrier between it and Allah."

Source: Riyad as-Salihin 1077 also in Bukhari and Muslim

A'isha, the wife of the Prophet, said:

"A group of Jews came to the Messenger of Allah, may Allah bless him and grant him peace, and said, "Poison ('sam' instead of 'salam') be upon you." 'A'isha said, "I understood it and said, 'And poison be upon you and the curse of Allah!' The Messenger of Allah, may Allah bless him and grant him peace, 'Easy, 'A'isha! Allah loves compassion in everything.' I said, 'Didn't you hear what they said?' The Messenger of Allah, replied, 'I already said, "and upon you".'"

Source: Al-Adab Al-Mufrad 462 Graded Sahih by Albani

Narrated Abu Sa`id Al-Khudri:

During the lifetime of the Prophet some people said, : O Allah's Messenger! Shall we see our Lord on the Day of Resurrection?" The Prophet said, "Yes; do you have any difficulty in seeing the sun at midday when it is bright and there is no cloud in the sky?" They replied, "No." He said, "Do you have any difficulty in seeing the moon on a full moon night when it is bright and there is no cloud in the sky?" They replied, "No." The Prophet said, "(Similarly) you will have no difficulty in seeing Allah on the Day of Resurrection as you have no difficulty in seeing either of them. On the Day of Resurrection, a call-maker will announce, "Let every nation follow that which they used to worship." Then none of those who used to worship anything other than Allah like idols and other deities but will fall in Hell (Fire), till there will remain none but those who used to worship Allah, both those who were obedient (i.e. good) and those who were disobedient (i.e. bad) and the remaining party of the people of the Scripture. Then the Jews will be called upon and it will be said to them, 'Who do you use to worship?' They will say, 'We used to worship Ezra, the son of Allah.' It will be said to them, 'You are liars, for Allah has never taken anyone as a wife or a son. What do you want now?' They will say, 'O our Lord! We are thirsty, so give us something to drink.' They will be directed and addressed thus, 'Will you drink,' whereupon they will be gathered unto Hell (Fire) which will look like a mirage whose different sides will be destroying each other. Then they will fall into the Fire. Afterwards the Christians will be called upon and it will be said to them, 'Who do you use to worship?' They will say, 'We used to worship Jesus, the son of Allah.' It will be said to them, 'You are liars, for Allah has never taken anyone as a wife or a son,' Then it will be said to them, 'What do you want?' They will say what the former people have said. Then, when there remain (in the gathering) none but those who used to worship Allah (Alone, the real Lord of the Worlds) whether they were obedient or disobedient. Then (Allah) the Lord of the worlds will come to them in a shape nearest to the picture they had in their minds about Him. It will be said, 'What are you waiting for?' Every nation have followed what they used to worship.' They will reply, 'We left the people in the world when we were in great need of them and we did not take them as friends. Now we are waiting for our Lord Whom we used to worship.' Allah will say, 'I am your Lord.' They will say twice or thrice, 'We do not worship any besides Allah.' "

Source: Sahih al-Bukhari 4581

Narrated `Umar:

I heard the Prophet saying, "Do not exaggerate in praising me as the Christians praised the son of Mary, for I am only a Slave. So, call me the Slave of Allah and His Apostle."

Source: Sahih al-Bukhari 3445

Abu Burda reported on the authority of his father that Allah's Apostle (ﷺ) said:

No Muslim would die but Allah would admit in his stead a Jew or a Christian in Hell-Fire. 'Umar b. Abd al-'Aziz took an oath: By One besides Whom there is no god but He, thrice that his father had narrated that to him from Allah's Messenger.

Source: Sahih Muslim 2767 b

It was narrated that Jabir bin 'Abdullah said:

"The Messenger of Allah said: 'Between a person and Kufr (disbelief) is abandoning the prayer.'"

Source: Sunan ibn Majah

English reference   : Vol. 1, Book 5, Hadith 1078

Graded Sahih by Darussalam

Narrated Ibn `Abbas:

Those who have made their Scripture into parts are the people of the Scripture who divided it into portions and believed in a part of it and disbelieved the other.

Source: Sahih al-Bukhari 4705

Narrated 'Adi bin Hatim:

"I came to the Prophet while I had a cross of gold around my neck. He said: 'O 'Adi! Remove this idol from yourself!' And I heard him reciting from Surah Bara'ah: They took their rabbis and monks as lords besides Allah (9:31). He said: 'As for them, they did not worship them, but when they made something lawful for them, they considered it lawful, and when they made something unlawful for them, they considered it unlawful.'"

Source: Jami at-Tirmidhi

English reference : Vol. 5, Book 44, Hadith 3095

Graded Daif by Darussalam

Narrated Nafi`:

Whenever Ibn `Umar was asked about marrying a Christian lady or a Jewess, he would say: "Allah has made it unlawful for the believers to marry ladies who ascribe partners in worship to Allah, and I do not know of a greater thing, as regards to ascribing partners in worship, etc. to Allah, than that a lady should say that Jesus is her Lord although he is just one of Allah's slaves."

Source: Sahih al-Bukhari 5285

It was narrated that Ibn 'Abbas said:

"There were kings after 'Isa(Jesus) bin Mariam who altered the Tawrah and the Injil, but there were among them believers who read the Tawrah. It was said to their kings: 'We have never heard of any slander worse than that of those (believers) who slander us and recite: "And whosoever does not judge by what Allah has revealed, such are the disbelievers." In these Verses, they are criticizing us for our deeds when they recite them.' So he called them together and gave them the choice between being put to death, or giving up reading the Tawrah and Injil, except for what had been altered. They said: 'Why do you want us to change?

Leave us alone.' Some of them said: 'Build us a tower and let us go up there, and give us something to lift up our food and drink so we do not have to mix with you.' Others said: 'Let us go and wander throughout the land, and we will drink as the wild animals drink, and if you capture us in your land, you may kill us.' Others said: 'Build houses for us in the wilderness, and we will dig wells and grow vegetables, and we will not mix with you or pass by you, for there is no one of the tribes among whom we do not have close relatives.' So they did that, and Allah revealed the words: 'But the monasticism which they invented for themselves, We did not prescribe for them, but (they sought it) only to please Allah therewith, but that they did not observe it with the right observance.' Then others said: 'We will worship as so-and-so worshipped, and we will wander as so-and-so wandered, and we will adopt houses (in the wilderness) as so-and-so did.' But they were still following their Shirk with no knowledge of the faith of those whom they claimed to be following. When Allah sent the Prophet, and they were only a few of them left, a man came down from his cell, and a wanderer came from his travels, and a monk came from his monastery, and they believed in him. And Allah said: 'O you who believe! Fear Allah, and believe in His Messenger , He will give you a double portion of His mercy - meaning, two rewards, because of their having believed in 'Isa and in the Tawrah and Injil, and for having believing in Muhammad; and He will give you a light by which you shall walk (straight), - meaning, the Qur'an, and their following the Prophet; and He said: 'So that the people of the Scripture (Jews and Christians) may know that they have no power whatsoever over the Grace of Allah.'"

Source: Sunan an-Nasa'i 5400 Graded Daif by Darussalam

Abdu'r-Rahman said

"Ibn 'Umar passed by a Christian who greeted him and Ibn 'Umar returned the greeting He was told that the man was a Christian. When he learned that, he went back to him and said, 'Give me back my greeting.'"

Source: Al-Adab Al-Mufrad 1115 Graded Hasan by Albani

It was narrated from Jaabir ibn 'Abdullah:

'Umar ibn al-Khattaab came to the Prophet (blessings and peace of Allah be upon him) with some written material he had got from one of the people of the Book. He read it to the Prophet, and he got angry and said: "Are you confused (about your religion), O son of al-Khattaab? By the One in Whose hand is my soul, I have brought it (the message of Islam) to you clear and pure. Do not ask them about anything, lest they tell you something true and you disbelieve it, or they tell you something false and you believe it. By the One in Whose hand is my soul, if Moosa were alive, he would have no option but to follow me."

Source: Musnad Ahmad 14736

Graded Hasan by al-Albaani in Irwa' al-Ghaleel, 6/34

Narrated Ubaidullah:

Ibn `Abbas said, "Why do you ask the people of the scripture about anything while your Book (Qur'an) which has been revealed to Allah's Messenger is newer and the latest? You read it pure, undistorted and unchanged, and Allah has told you that the people of the scripture (Jews and Christians) changed their scripture and distorted it, and wrote the scripture with their own hands and said, 'It is from Allah,' to sell it for a little gain. Does not the knowledge which has come to you prevent you from asking them about anything? No, by Allah, we have never seen any man from them asking you regarding what has been revealed to you!"

Source: Sahih al-Bukhari 7363

Fatwas proving the Kufr of Christians and Jews

https://islamqa.info/en/answers/21249/kufr-and-its-various-kinds

Question

I read in Question no. 12811 that there are various kinds of major kufr that puts one beyond the pale of Islam. I hope that you could explain that and give some examples of it.

Answer

Praise be to Allah.

The reality of kufr and its various kinds is a lengthy topic, but we may sum it up in the following points:

1 – The importance of knowing what kufr is and the forms it may take:

The texts of the Qur'aan and Sunnah indicate that faith is not valid and is not accepted unless two conditions are met – which are what are implied by the testimony that there is no god except Allaah. These two conditions are submission to Allaah alone (Tawheed), and denouncing and shunning all kinds of kufr and shirk.

A person cannot denounce or shun anything unless he knows what it is. From this we understand the importance of knowing what Tawheed is, so that we may act accordingly and attain Tawheed, and knowing what kufr and shirk is so that we may avoid them and steer clear of them.

2 – Definition of kufr:

Kufr in Arabic means covering and concealing something.

In shar'i terminology it means "not believing in Allaah and His Messenger, whether that is accompanied by denial or it is not accompanied by denial but rather doubt, or turning away from faith out of jealousy or arrogance, or because one is following whims and desires that prevent one from following the message. So kufr is the attribute of everyone who rejects something that Allaah has commanded us to believe in, after news of that has reached him, whether he rejects it in his heart without uttering it, or he speaks those words of rejection without believing it in his heart, or he does both; or he does an action which is described in the texts as putting one beyond the pale of faith." See Majmoo' al-Fataawa by Shaykh al-Islam Ibn Taymiyah, 12/335; al-Ihkaam fi Usool al-Ahkaam by Ibn Hazam, 1/45.

Ibn Hazam said in his book al-Fasl: "Rejecting something for which there is sound proof that there can be no faith without believing in it is kufr, and uttering words for which there is proof that uttering them is kufr is kufr. Doing any action for which there is proof that it is kufr is also kufr."

3 – Kinds of major kufr which put one beyond the pale of Islam

The scholars divided kufr into a number of categories, under which they listed many forms and kinds of shirk. These are as follows:

-1-

The kufr of denial and rejection. This kufr may sometimes take the form of disbelief in the heart – which occurs rarely among the kuffaar, as Ibn al-Qayyim (may Allaah have mercy on him) said – and sometimes it takes the form of outward or apparent rejection, which means concealing the truth and not submitting to it outwardly, whilst recognizing it and knowing it inwardly, such as the Jews' rejection of Muhammad (peace and blessings of Allaah be upon him). Allaah says of them (interpretation of the meaning):

"then when there came to them that which they had recognized, they disbelieved in it" [al-Baqarah 2:89]

He also said (interpretation of the meaning]:

"But verily, a party of them conceal the truth while they know it"

[al-Baqarah 2:146]

That is because rejection only happens which a person knows the truth and refuses it. Hence Allaah stated that the kuffaar's disbelief in the Messenger (peace and blessings of Allaah be upon him) was not disbelief in the true sense of the word, because their disbelief was only outward and verbal, and inwardly they recognized the truth.

Allaah says (interpretation of the meaning):

"it is not you that they deny, but it is the Verses (the Qur'aan) of Allaah that the Zaalimoon (polytheists and wrongdoers) deny"

[al-An'aam 6:33]

"And they belied them (those Ayaat) wrongfully and arrogantly, though their ownselves were convinced thereof"

[al-Naml 27:14]

Similar to this is the kufr of permitting that which is forbidden. Whoever regards as permissible something which he knows that Islam has forbidden has disbelieved in the Messenger (peace and blessings of Allaah be upon him) and in that which he brought. The same applies to one who forbids something which he knows that Islam has permitted.

-2-

The kufr of turning away in arrogance, such as the kufr of Iblees of whom Allaah said:

"... except Iblees (Satan), he refused and was proud and was one of the disbelievers (disobedient to Allaah)"

[al-Baqarah 2:34 – interpretation of the meaning]

And Allaah says (interpretation of the meaning):

"They (hypocrites) say: 'We have believed in Allaah and in the Messenger (Muhammad), and we obey,' then a party of them turn away thereafter, such are not believers"

[al-Noor 24:47]

So Allaah has stated that those who do not act in accordance with faith are not believers, even if they utter the words of faith. The kufr of turning away means that one ignores the truth and does not learn it or act in accordance with it, whether it is the matter of words, actions or beliefs. Allaah says (interpretation of the meaning):

"*But those who disbelieve, turn away from that whereof they are warned*"[al-Ahqaaf 46:3]

Whoever turns away verbally from that which the Messenger has brought is like one who says "I will not follow him." The one who turns away by his actions is like one who runs away from hearing the truth which he brought, or puts his fingers in his ears so as not to hear, or who hears it but turns away in his heart and refuses to believe, and who refuses to act upon it. He has disbelieved in the sense of the kufr of turning away.

-3-

The kufr of hypocrisy. This takes the form of not believing in the heart and not acting, whilst submitting outwardly in order to show off to people. This is like the kufr of Ibn Salool and the other munaafiqeen (hypocrites) of whom Allaah said (interpretation of the meaning):

"*And of mankind, there are some (hypocrites) who say: 'We believe in Allaah and the Last Day,' while in fact they believe not.*

They (think to) deceive Allaah and those who believe, while they only deceive themselves, and perceive (it) not!

In their hearts is a disease (of doubt and hypocrisy) and Allaah has increased their disease. A painful torment is theirs because they used to tell lies.

And when it is said to them: 'Make not mischief on the earth,' they say: 'We are only peacemakers.'

Verily, they are the ones who make mischief, but they perceive not.

And when it is said to them (hypocrites): 'Believe as the people (followers of Muhammad, Al-Ansaar and Al-Muhajiroon) have believed,' they say: 'Shall we believe as the fools have believed?' Verily, they are the fools, but they know not.

And when they meet those who believe, they say: 'We believe,' but when they are alone with their Shayaateen (devils — polytheists, hypocrites), they say: 'Truly, we are with you; verily, we were but mocking.'

Allaah mocks at them and gives them increase in their wrong-doing to wander blindly.

These are they who have purchased error for guidance, so their commerce was profitless. And they were not guided.

Their likeness is as the likeness of one who kindled a fire; then, when it lighted all around him, Allaah took away their light and left them in darkness. (So) they could not see.

They are deaf, dumb, and blind, so they return not (to the Right Path).

Or like a rainstorm from the sky, wherein is darkness, thunder, and lightning. They thrust their fingers in their ears to keep out the stunning thunderclap for fear of death. But Allaah ever encompasses the disbelievers (i.e. Allaah will gather them all together).

The lightning almost snatches away their sight, whenever it flashes for them, they walk therein, and when darkness covers them, they stand still. And if Allaah willed, He could have taken away their hearing and their sight. Certainly, Allaah has power over all things"

[al-Baqarah 2:8-20]

-4-

The kufr of doubt, which means hesitating with regard to following the truth and being uncertain as to whether it is true, because what is required is certainty of faith (yaqeen) that what the Messenger brought is truth with no hint of doubt in it. Whoever thinks that what he brought may not be true has disbelieved, in the sense of kufr of doubt, as Allaah says (interpretation of the meaning):

"And he went into his garden while in a state (of pride and disbelief), unjust to himself. He said: 'I think not that this will ever perish.

And I think not the Hour will ever come, and if indeed I am brought back to my Lord, (on the Day of Resurrection), I surely, shall find better than this when I return to Him.'

His companion said to him during the talk with him: 'Do you disbelieve in Him Who created you out of dust (i.e. your father Adam), then out of Nutfah (mixed semen drops of male and female discharge), then fashioned you into a man?

But as for my part, (I believe) that He is Allaah, my Lord, and none shall I associate as partner with my Lord.'"

[al-Kahf 18:35-38]

From this we may conclude that kufr – which is the opposite of eemaan or faith – may take the form of feelings in the heart, such as hating Allaah or His signs, or His Messenger (peace and blessings of Allaah be upon him); this contradicts love and faith which support the actions of the heart. Kufr may also take the form of spoken words, such as insulting Allaah, or it may be an outward action, such as prostrating to idols, or offering sacrifices to someone other than Allaah. Just as faith takes the form of actions of the heart, words on the tongue and outward physical actions, so too kufr may take the form of actions of the heart, words on the tongue and outward physical actions. We ask Allaah to keep us safe from kufr and its branches, and to increase us in faith and make us guided and cause us to guide others… Ameen.

And Allaah knows best.

https://islamqa.info/en/answers/12811/the-misguidance-of-those-who-believe-that-kufr-only-means-disbelief

Question

Is the idea that kufr is only disbelief an idea that came from the Murji'ah sect?

Answer

Praise be to Allah.

Kufr takes different forms. The Murji'ah and other followers of bid'ah (reprehensible innovation) say that kufr is only based on disbelief. But this view is contrary to the evidence and contrary to the truth. It is known that the Messengers were sent with miracles and proof to which hearts submitted. It is rare indeed that people believed that what the Prophets brought was false; most instances of kufr stemmed from arrogance, rejection and stubbornness. Allaah mentioned that Quraysh did not disbelieve the Prophet (peace and blessings of Allaah be upon him), *"but it is the*

[113]

Verses (the Qur'aan) of Allaah that the Zaalimoon (polytheists and wrongdoers) deny" [al-An'aam 6:33 – interpretation of the meaning]. This happens very often. Hence the scholars divided kufr into various types: the kufr of negligence and not caring; the kufr of arrogance and pride; the kufr of disbelief; the kufr of hypocrisy; the kufr of doubt. There is a great deal of evidence to that effect in the Book of Allaah and the Sunnah of His Messenger (peace and blessings of Allaah be upon him). The story of Abu Taalib and the Prophet (peace and blessings of Allaah be upon him) is clear; he believed in him and he used to say, "Our son does not tell lies," but he was still a kaafir, because he never made a statement of faith or followed it up with actions.

https://islamqa.info/en/answers/67626/the-difference-between-the-mushrikeen-and-the-kuffaar-and-to-which-category-do-the-jews-and-christians-belong

Question

What is the difference between mushrikeen and kuffaar? Are the Jews and Christians mushrikeen or kuffaar?

Answer

Praise be to Allah.

Firstly:

The kaafir is the one who denies and conceals the truth. The basic meaning of the word kufr in Arabic is concealment. Shirk means devoting worship to anyone or anything other than Allaah.

Kufr may take the form of denying and rejecting, but the mushrik may also believe in Allaah. This is the difference between the mushrik and the kaafir.

Each word may also carry the meaning of the other, so the word kufr may be used in the sense of shirk, and the word shirk may be used in the sense of kufr.

Al-Nawawi (may Allaah have mercy on him) said:

Kufr and shirk may carry the same meaning, which is disbelief in Allaah, may He be exalted, or they may be used separately, whereby shirk refers to the worship of idols and other created beings, whilst also acknowledging Allaah, as the kuffaar of Quraysh did, and kufr may have a more general meaning than shirk. End quote.

Sharh Saheeh Muslim. 2/71

Shaykh 'Abd al-'Azeez ibn Baaz (may Allaah have mercy on him) said:

Kufr is denial and concealment of the truth, such as one who denies that prayer is obligatory, or that zakaah is obligatory, or that fasting Ramadaan is obligatory, or that doing Hajj when one is able to is obligatory, or that honouring one's parents is obligatory, and so on, or one who denies that zina is haraam, or that drinking intoxicants is haraam, or that disobeying one's parents is haraam, and so on.

Shirk is devoting acts of worship to something or someone other than Allaah, such as one who seeks the help of the dead, those who are absent, the jinn, idols, the stars, and so on, or who offers sacrifices to them, or makes vows to them.

[115]

A kaafir may be called a mushrik and a mushrik may be called a kaafir, as Allaah says (interpretation of the meaning):

"And whoever invokes (or worships), besides Allaah, any other ilaah (god), of whom he has no proof; then his reckoning is only with his Lord. Surely, Al-Kaafiroon (the disbelievers in Allaah and in the Oneness of Allaah, polytheists, pagans, idolaters) will not be successful" [al-Mu'minoon 23:117]

"Verily, whosoever sets up partners (in worship) with Allaah, then Allaah has forbidden Paradise to him, and the Fire will be his abode" [al-Maa'idah 5:72]

And Allaah says in Soorat Faatir (interpretation of the meaning):

"Such is Allaah, your Lord; His is the kingdom. And those, whom you invoke or call upon instead of Him, own not even a Qitmeer (the thin membrane over the date stone). 14. If you invoke (or call upon) them, they hear not your call; and if (in case) they were to hear, they could not grant it (your request) to you. And on the Day of Resurrection, they will disown your worshipping them. And none can inform you (O Muhammad) like Him Who is the All-Knower (of everything)"
[Faatir 35:13-14]

Their calling on anything other than Allaah is called shirk in this soorah, but in Soorat al-Mu'minoon it is called kufr.

Allaah says in Soorat al-Tawbah (interpretation of the meaning):

"They (the disbelievers, the Jews and the Christians) want to extinguish Allaah's Light (with which Muhammad has been sent

— Islamic Monotheism) with their mouths, but Allaah will not allow except that His Light should be perfected even though the Kaafiroon (disbelievers) hate (it). 33. It is He Who has sent His Messenger (Muhammad) with guidance and the religion of truth (Islam), to make it superior over all religions even though the Mushrikoon (polytheists, pagans, idolaters, disbelievers in the Oneness of Allaah) hate (it)"

[al-Tawbah 9:32-33]

Here Allaah calls the kuffaar kuffaar, and He calls them mushrikeen. This indicates that a kaafir may be called a mushrik and a mushrik may be called a kaafir. There are many similar verses and ahaadeeth.

Another example is the hadeeth in which the Prophet (peace and blessings of Allaah be upon him) said: "Between a man and shirk and kufr there stands his giving up prayer." Narrated by Muslim in his Saheeh from Jaabir ibn 'Abd-Allaah (may Allaah be pleased with him). And the Prophet (peace and blessings of Allaah be upon him) said: "The covenant that differentiates us from them is prayer; whoever gives it up is a kaafir." Narrated by Imam Ahmad, Abu Dawood, al-Tirmidhi, al-Nasaa'i and Ibn Maajah with a saheeh isnaad from Buraydah ibn al-Husayb (may Allaah be pleased with him). And Allaah is the Source of strength. End quote.

Majmoo' Fataawa al-Shaykh Ibn Baaz, 9/174, 175.

The Shaykh (may Allaah have mercy on him) also said:

It is also shirk to worship only something other than Allaah. This is called shirk, and it is called kufr. Whoever turns

away from Allaah altogether and devotes his worship to
something other than Allaah, such as trees, rocks, idols, the
jinn or some of the dead such as those whom they call
awliya' ("saints"), and worship them, pray to them or fast
for them, and forget Allaah altogether, this is the worst form
of kufr and shirk. We ask Allaah to keep us safe and sound.
Similarly those who deny the existence of Allaah and say
that there is no god, that life is only material, such as the
communists and atheists, are the most disbelieving and
misguided of people, and the worst in terms of shirk. We ask
Allaah to keep us safe and sound. The point is that people
who hold these and similar beliefs are all regarded as
mushrikeen and kaafirs who disbelieve in Allaah. Some
people, out of ignorance, mistakenly regard calling upon the
dead and seeking their help as waseelah and think that it is
permissible. This is a serious error, because this action is one
of the worst forms of shirk and associating others with
Allaah. Some ignorant people and mushrikeen call it
waseelah, but it is the religion of the mushrikeen whom
Allaah criticized and condemned. He sent the Messenger
and revealed His Books to denounce it and warn against it.
End quote.

Majmoo' Fataawa al-Shaykh Ibn Baaz, 4/32, 33

Secondly:

The Jews and Christians are both kaafirs and mushrikeen.
They are kaafirs because they deny the truth and reject it.
And they are mushrikeen because they worship someone
other than Allaah.

Allaah says (interpretation of the meaning):

"And the Jews say: 'Uzair (Ezra) is the son of Allaah, and the Christians say: Messiah is the son of Allaah. That is their saying with their mouths, resembling the saying of those who disbelieved aforetime. Allaah's Curse be on them, how they are deluded away from the truth! 31. They (Jews and Christians) took their rabbis and their monks to be their lords besides Allaah (by obeying them in things which they made lawful or unlawful according to their own desires without being ordered by Allaah), and (they also took as their Lord) Messiah, son of Maryam (Mary), while they (Jews and Christians) were commanded [in the Tawraat (Torah) and the Injeel (Gospel)] to worship none but One Ilaah (God — Allaah) Laa ilaaha illa Huwa (none has the right to be worshipped but He). Praise and glory be to Him (far above is He) from having the partners they associate (with Him)"

[al-Tawbah 9:30, 31]

Here they are described as mushrikeen. In Soorat al-Bayyinah they are described as kaafirs, as Allaah says (interpretation of the meaning):

"Those who disbelieve from among the people of the Scripture (Jews and Christians) and Al-Mushrikoon, were not going to leave (their disbelief) until there came to them clear evidence"

[al-Bayyinah 98:1]

Shaykh 'Abd al-'Azeez ibn Baaz (may Allaah have mercy on him) said, refuting those who say that the word mushrikeen cannot be applied to the People of the Book:

It is most likely that the people of the Book are included among the mushrikeen, men and women alike, when this word is used in general terms. because the kuffaar are undoubtedly mushrikeen. Hence they are forbidden to enter al-Masjid al-Haraam, because Allaah says (interpretation of the meaning):

"O you who believe (in Allaah's Oneness and in His Messenger Muhammad)! Verily, the Mushrikoon (polytheists, pagans, idolaters, disbelievers in the Oneness of Allaah, and in the Message of Muhammad) are Najasun (impure). So let them not come near Al-Masjid Al-Haraam (at Makkah) after this year"

[al-Tawbah 9:28]

If the People of the Book did not come under the general heading of mushrikeen, then this verse would not apply to them, and Allaah would not have referred to the beliefs of the Jews and Christians in Soorat Baraa'ah (al-Tawbah) where He says (interpretation of the meaning):

"they (Jews and Christians) were commanded [in the Tawraat (Torah) and the Injeel (Gospel)] to worship none but One Ilaah (God — Allaah) Laa ilaaha illa Huwa (none has the right to be worshipped but He). Praise and glory be to Him (far above is He) from having the partners they associate (with Him)"

[al-Tawbah 9:31]

So they are all described as mushrikeen, because the Jews said that 'Uzayr is the son of God and the Christians said that the Messiah is the son of God; and because they took their priests and rabbis as lords instead of Allaah. All of this is the worst form of shirk. And there are many similar verses. End quote.

Majmoo' Fataawa al-Shaykh Ibn Baaz, 4/274

And Allaah knows best.

https://islamqa.info/en/answers/4322/if-a-jew-or-christian-believes-that-allaah-is-one-but-does-not-rule-according-to-the-quraan

Question

If today there is a jew or a christian who believes in Alaah and that he has no partner. He believes in the prophethood of the Messenger of Allaah . But he does not rule by the Qur'aan even though he accepts it as being from Allaah, but he deems it permissible to rule by the original torah. Is he a muslim. This needs a quick response if you can , for dawah purposes. Jazak Allaahu Khair.

Answer

Praise be to Allah.

We sent this question to our Shaykh 'Abd al-Rahmaan al-Barraak, who replied as follows:

Praise be to Allaah. Among the basic principles of faith are Belief in all the Books that have been revealed from Allaah, and belief in all the Messengers. These two principles include belief in the noblest of Books, which is the Qur'aan, and the best of the Messengers, namely Muhammad (peace and blessings of Allaah be upon him), the Seal of the Messengers and the Messenger of Allaah to all of mankind from the time when Allaah sent him until the time when the Hour will begin. Every person from every nation must believe in him and follow him and rule by his sharee'ah (laws). Whoever claims to believe in him and in the Qur'aan, but does not rule according to it or follow him in everything that he brought and believe everything he told us, is not a Muslim or a believer. If he dies like this then he will be one of the people of Hell. If he claims to believe in Allaah Alone, with no partner or associate, and in all the Messengers, belief in the Messenger and in the Qur'aan does not only mean believing that they are true, without following them and ruling according to what they say. Many of the Mushrikeen believed in the Messenger of Allaah (peace and blessings of Allaah be upon him) in their hearts, and there were those who believed in him in their hearts and in the words they spoke, but this did not benefit them at all, like his uncle Abu Taalib. This belief did not help them at all when they insisted on not following. Similarly, the Jews and Christians who knew him as they knew their sons, and who admitted that they believed in the Messenger (peace and blessings of Allaah be upon him), but this knowledge and belief did not benefit them at all when they refused to follow him. They were kaafirs and Allaah decreed their blood and their wealth to be permissible for His Messenger (peace and blessings of Allaah be upon him), so he fought them, and Allaah caused him to prevail over them, and His religion to prevail over all other religions. Allaah says (interpretation of the meaning):

"It is He Who has sent His Messenger (Muhammad (peace and blessings of Allaah be upon him)) with guidance and the religion of truth (islam), to make it superior over all religions, even though the Mushrikoon (polytheists, pagans, idolaters, disbelievers in the Oneness of Allaah) hate (it)." [al-Tawbah 9:33]

So every Jew and Christian has to enter the religion of Islam which Allaah revealed to His Prophet Muhammad (peace and blessings of Allaah be upon him), because the Message of Muhammad is the final Message, which abrogates the previous religions. Allaah says (interpretation of the meaning):

"And whoever seeks a religion other than islam, it will never be accepted of him" [Aal 'Imraan 3:85]

According to a saheeh hadeeth: *"By the One in Whose hand is the soul of Muhammad, there is no one among this ummah, Jew or Christian, who hears of me than dies without believing in that with which I have been sent, but he will be one of the people of Hellfire."* (Reported by Muslim, 218).

On this basis, the religion of any Jew or Christian will not be correct unless he believes in the sharee'ah of Islam and adheres to the rulings of the Qur'aan. The Qur'aan is Muhaymin (i.e., it testifies to the truth that is in the previous scriptures and exposes the falsehood that has been added to them), and it abrogates the previous Books. The Tawraat (Torah) and Injeel have been abrogated and have been changed and altered. And Allaah knows best.

https://islamqa.info/en/answers/2912/who-are-the-jews-and-christians-who-will-enter-paradise

Question

For the time being, I do not have the resources to quote the exact Quranic verse, nor can I tell you what sura it has been taken from. However, I believe it is a common verse. I understand little Arabic; hence I found that in English. The verse can be interpretted as such:

The godfearing Jews, muslims and christians will not have fear (on that day).
I am not exactly sure of the bracketted phrase.
Now my question to you: is it mistranliteration?
We know that christians and jews in general cannot be hoped to have any sanction in the life hereafter. So, how do we understand the verse?

Answer

Praise be to Allah.

What you refer to in your question is mentioned in two similar aayaat in the Qur'aan. The first of them is the aayah (interpretation of the meaning): "Verily, those who believe and those who are Jews and Christians, and Sabians, whoever believes in Allaah and the Last Day and do righteous good deeds shall have their reward with their Lord, on them shall be no fear, nor shall they grieve." [al-Baqarah 2:62]

The second is the aayah (interpretation of the meaning): *"Surely, those who believe, those who are the Jews and the Sabians and the Christians – whosoever believed in Allaah and the Last Day, and worked righteousness, on them shall be no fear, nor shall they grieve."* [al-Maa'idah 5:69]

In order to understand these aayaat correctly, we need to refer to the scholars of Tafseer (Qur'aanic commentary). The great Imaam Ismaa'eel ibn Katheer, may Allaah have mercy on him, said in his tafseer of the aayah from Soorat al-Baqarah:

"Allaah, may He be exalted, points out that whoever of the previous nations did well and was obedient, will have a good reward, and this will be the case for everyone who follows the Unlettered Prophet [Prophet Muhammad (peace and blessings of Allaah be upon him) until the Hour comes – he will have eternal happiness, and they will not fear what they are going to face, nor will they grieve for what they have left behind. As Allaah says (interpretation of the meaning): 'No doubt! Verily, the awliya' of Allaah [i.e., those who believe in the Oneness of Allaah and fear Allaah much, and love Allaah much], no fear shall come upon them nor shall they grieve.' [Yoonus 10:62]. And Allaah tells us what the angels say to the believers at the time of death (interpretation of the meaning): 'Verily, those who say, "Our Lord is Allaah," then they istaqaamu [stood straight, i.e., truly followed Islam], on them the angels will descend (at the time of their death) (saying): "Fear not, nor grieve! But receive the glad tidings of Paradise which you have been promised!"' [Fussilat 41:30]

As far as the Jews are concerning, their faith meant believing in the Tawraat (original Torah) and following the way of Moosa (peace be upon him) until 'Eesa came, after which whoever continued to follow the Torah and the way of Moosa, and did not leave this and follow 'Eesa, was doomed. As far as the Christians are concerned, their faith meant believing in the Injeel (original Gospel) and following the laws of 'Eesa; whoever did this was a believer whose faith was acceptable to Allaah, until Muhammad (peace and blessings of Allaah be upon him) came, after which whoever did not follow Muhammad (peace and blessings of Allaah be upon him) and leave the way of 'Eesa and the Injeel that he had been following before, was doomed.

The aayah (interpretation of the meaning), "And whoever seeks a religion other than Islam, it will never be accepted of him, and in the Hereafter he will be one of the losers" [Aal 'Imraan 3:85] is a statement that Allaah will not accept any way or deed from anyone, after sending His Final Messenger, except those that are in accordance with the laws of Muhammad (peace and blessings of Allaah be upon him). Prior to this, however, anyone who followed the Prophet of his own time was on the Straight Path of salvation. So the Jews were those who followed Moosa (peace be upon him) and referred to the Tawraat for judgement at that time. When Allaah sent 'Eesa (peace be upon him), the Children of Israel were obliged to follow him and obey him, and so they and others who followed him became Christians.. When Allaah sent Muhammad (peace and blessings of Allaah be upon him), as the Final Prophet and a Messenger to all the children of Adam, all of mankind was obliged to believe in him and obey him, and refrain from what he prohibited. Those who did so are the true believers. The ummah (nation) of Muhammad (peace and blessings of Allaah be upon him) are called the believers because of their deep eemaan (faith) and conviction, and because they believe in all the past Prophets and in the prophesied events that are yet to come."

Commenting on the aayah in Soorat al-Baqarah, Ibn Katheer (may Allaah have mercy on him) said:

"What is meant is that every group believed in Allaah and the Last Day, which is the appointed Day of Reckoning, and did righteous deeds. But after Muhammad (peace and blessings of Allaah be upon him) was sent to both mankind and the jinn, true belief can only be in accordance with the way of Muhammad (peace and blessings of Allaah be upon him). Whoever follows his way will not fear the future or grieve for what they leave behind.

https://islamqa.info/en/answers/14296/consequences-for-one-who-does-not-adhere-to-islam

Question

What are the consequences for one who does not adhere to Islam?

Answer

Praise be to Allah.

As you know, Islam is the religion of Allaah, and it is the true religion. It is the religion which was brought by all the Prophets and Messengers. Allaah has prepared a great reward in this world and in the hereafter for those who believe in it, and He has prepared a severe punishment for those who disbelieve in it.

Allaah is the Creator and Sovereign, the One Who is in control of this universe, and you, O man, are part of His creation; He has subjugated to you all that is in the universe, and has prescribed His laws for you, which He has commanded you to follow. If you believe and obey what He has commanded you and keep away from what He has prohibited to you, then you will attain that eternal bliss which He has promised you in the Hereafter, and you will be happy in this world because of the different kinds of blessings which He will bestow upon you, and you will be akin to the most wise of creation and the purest in heart, namely the Prophets, Messengers, righteous and angels who are close to Allaah.

But if you disbelieve and disobey your Lord, you will lose in this world and in the Hereafter. You will be exposed to His wrath and punishment in this world and in the Hereafter. You will be akin to the most evil and foolish of creation, and worse than the devils, wrongdoers, evildoers and false gods. This is in general terms.

I will explain to you something about the consequences of kufr, the details of which are as follows:

1 – Fear and lack of security

Allaah has promised those who believe in Him and follow His Messengers complete security in this world and in the Hereafter. He says (interpretation of the meaning):

"It is those who believe (in the Oneness of Allaah and worship none but Him Alone) and confuse not their Belief with Zulm (wrong, i.e. by worshipping others besides Allaah), for them (only) there is security and they are the guided"

[al-An'aam 6:82]

Allaah is al-Mu'min (the Giver of security) and al-Muhaymin (the Watcher over His creatures); He is the Sovereign of all that exists in the universe. If Allaah loves a person for his faith then He will grant him security, tranquility and contentment. If a man disbelieves in Him He will take away his tranquility and security, so you will only see him either fearful about his destiny in the Hereafter, or fearing sickness for himself, or fearing for his future in this world. This is why the insurance business was established, to insure people's lives and property, because of the lack of security and the lack of trust in Allaah.

2 – A life of hardship

Allaah has created man and has subjugated to him all that is in the universe. He has decreed for every creature its share of provision and its life span. So you see the bird going out from its nest in the morning to seek its provision, which it picks up, flying from branch to branch and singing the most beautiful songs. Man is one of these creatures whose provision and lifespan is already allocated. If he believes in his Lord and adheres to His laws, He will bless him with happiness and stability, and make things easy for him, even if he is only given the bare necessities of life.

But if he disbelieves in Him, and arrogantly refuses to worship him, He will make his life hard and fill him with worries and distress, even if he possesses all kinds of comforts and luxuries. Do you not see how many suicides in the world are committed by people who have all kinds of luxuries? Do you not see the extravagant spending on furniture and travel aimed at enjoying life? What makes people spend extravagantly is the fact that their hearts are devoid of faith, and their feeling that life is difficult and hard; it is an attempt to rid themselves of these feelings by ever-changing means. Allaah indeed spoke the truth when He said:

"But whosoever turns away from My Reminder (i.e. neither believes in this Qur'aan nor acts on its teachings) verily, for him is a life of hardship, and We shall raise him up blind on the Day of Resurrection"

[Ta-Ha 20:124]

3 – He will live in conflict with himself and with the universe around him

That is because his own soul was created to believe in and worship Allaah alone (i.e., Tawheed). Allaah says:

"Allaah's Fitrah (i.e. Allaah's Islamic Monotheism) with which He has created mankind" [al-Room 30:30]

His body submits to its Creator, and acts in accordance with His system, but the kaafir insists on going against his own innate nature and lives in such a way that in matters where he is given a choice, he always chooses to follow the way which goes against the command of his Lord, so even if his body is surrendering to the laws of Allaah, in matters of choice he chooses to oppose the laws of Allaah.

He is in a state of conflict with the universe around him, because this entire universe, from the hugest galaxies to the tiniest insect is operating in accordance with the laws that Allaah has decreed for it. Allaah says (interpretation of the meaning):

"Then He rose over (Istawa) towards the heaven when it was smoke, and said to it and to the earth: 'Come both of you willingly or unwillingly.' They both said: 'We come willingly'"

[Fussilat 41:11]

Indeed, this universe loves the one who also submits to Allaah, and it hates the one who goes against that. The kaafir is the rebellious one in this universe, where he sets himself up in opposition to his Lord, rallying others to oppose Him too. Hence it comes as no surprise that the heavens and the earth and all creatures hate him and hate his kufr and heresy. Allaah says (interpretation of the meaning):

"And they say: 'The Most Gracious (Allaah) has begotten a son (or offspring or children) [as the Jews say: 'Uzayr (Ezra) is the son of Allaah, and the Christians say that He has begotten a son ['Eesa (Jesus)], and the pagan Arabs say that He has begotten daughters (angels and others)].' Indeed you have brought forth (said) a terrible evil thing. Whereby the heavens are almost torn, and the earth is split asunder, and the mountains fall in ruins, That they ascribe a son (or offspring or children) to the Most Gracious (Allaah). But it is not suitable for (the Majesty of) the Most Gracious (Allaah) that He should beget a son (or offspring or children). There is none in the heavens and the earth but comes unto the Most Gracious (Allaah) as a slave" [Maryam 19:88-93]

And Allaah says of Pharaoh and his troops:

"And the heavens and the earth wept not for them, nor were they given a respite" [al-Dukhaan 44:29]

4 – He will live in ignorance

For kufr is ignorance, indeed it is the greatest form of ignorance, because the kaafir is ignorant of his Lord and he sees this universe that He created in such an amazing way, and he sees how great is his own creation, then he ignores the One Who created this universe and Who created him. Is this not the greatest form of ignorance?

5 – He will wrong himself and wrong those around him

Because he is subjugating himself to something other than that for which he was created, and because he does not worship his Lord, rather he worships someone other than Him. Wrongdoing means putting something in the wrong place, and what wrongdoing is greater than directing worship to someone other than the One Who deserves it? Luqmaan the Wise said, explaining the abhorrent nature of shirk:

"O my son! Join not in worship others with Allaah. Verily, joining others in worship with Allaah is a great Zulm (wrong) indeed"

[Luqmaan 31:13 – interpretation of the meaning]

He also does wrong to others around him, humans and other creatures, because he does not recognize the rights of those who have rights. When the Day of Resurrection comes, everyone whom he wronged, whether human or animal, will stand before him and will ask his Lord to settle the score between them.

6 – He exposes himself to the wrath and anger of Allaah in this world

He is exposed to that because disasters and calamities will befall him, as a punishment in this world. Allaah says (interpretation of the meaning):

"Do then those who devise evil plots feel secure that Allaah will not sink them into the earth, or that the torment will not seize them from directions they perceive not?

Or that He may catch them in the midst of their going to and fro (in their jobs), so that there be no escape for them (from Allaah's punishment)?"

[al-Nahl 16:45-46]

"And a disaster will not cease to strike those who disbelieved because of their (evil) deeds or it (i.e. the disaster) settles close to their homes, until the Promise of Allaah comes to pass. Certainly, Allaah breaks not His Promise"

[al-Ra'd 13:31]

"Or, did the people of the towns then feel secure against the coming of Our punishment in the forenoon while they were playing?"

[al-A'raaf 7:98]

This is the situation of everyone who turns away from the remembrance of Allaah. Allaah said, telling us of the punishments that befall the earlier disbelieving nations (interpretation of the meaning):

"So We punished each (of them) for his sins, of them were some on whom We sent Haasib (a violent wind with shower of stones) [as on the people of Loot (Lot)], and of them were some who were overtaken by As-Sayhah [torment — awful cry, (as Thamood or Shu'ayb's people)], and of them were some whom We caused the earth to swallow [as Qaaroon (Korah)], and of them were some whom We drowned [as the people of Nooh (Noah), or Fir'awn (Pharaoh) and his people]. It was not Allaah Who wronged them, but they wronged themselves"

[al-'Ankaboot 29:40]

And you see the disasters around you that have befallen people as a punishment and vengeance from Allaah.

7 – Disappointment and loss are decreed for him

Because of his wrongdoing he will lose out on the greatest things that hearts and souls can enjoy, which is knowing Allaah and conversing with Him, and finding peace and contentment in Him. He will lose in this world because he will live a life of misery and confusion therein, and he will lose his own soul for the sake of which he has been striving, because he did not subjugate it to the purpose for which it was created. He will not be happy in this world, because his soul lives a miserable life and dies a miserable death, and it will be resurrected with the doomed. Allaah says (interpretation of the meaning):

"And as for those whose Scale will be light, they are those who will lose their ownselves (by entering Hell)" [al-A'raaf 7:9]

And he will lose his family, because he lives with them in a state of disbelief in Allaah, so they are the same as him in their misery and hard life, and their ultimate destiny will be the Fire. Allaah says (interpretation of the meaning):

"The losers are those who will lose themselves and their families on the Day of Resurrection" [al-Zumar 39:15, al-Shoora 42:45]

On the Day of Resurrection they will be gathered into Hell, what an evil abode. Allaah says (interpretation of the meaning):

"(It will be said to the angels): 'Assemble those who did wrong, together with their companions (from the devils) and what they

used to worship, Instead of Allaah, and lead them on to the way of flaming Fire (Hell)'"

[al-Saaffaat 37:22-23]

He lives disbelieving in his Lord and denying His blessings

Allaah created him from nothing, and bestowed all kinds of blessings upon him. How can he then worship someone other than Him, and take as a friend someone other than Him, and give thanks to someone other than Him? What denial can be greater or more abhorrent than this?

9 – He will be deprived of true life

That is because the one who deserves a good life is the one who believes in his Lord and knows his purpose in life, who knows where he is going and is certain that he will be resurrected. So he acknowledges the rights of all those who have rights, and he does not deny any rights, or harm any other creature. He lives the life of the blessed and enjoys a good life in this world and in the Hereafter. Allaah says:

"Whoever works righteousness – whether male or female – while he (or she) is a true believer (of Islamic Monotheism) verily, to him We will give a good life" [al-Nahl 16:97]

"and pleasant dwellings in 'Adn (Eden) Paradise; that is indeed the great success" [al-Saff 61:12]

As for the one who lives a life akin to that of the animals, not knowing his Lord or knowing his aim in life or where he is headed, rather his aim is to eat, drink and sleep ... what difference is there between him and the rest of the animals?

Indeed, he is further astray. Allaah says (interpretation of the meaning):

"And surely, We have created many of the jinn and mankind for Hell. They have hearts wherewith they understand not, and they have eyes wherewith they see not, and they have ears wherewith they hear not (the truth). They are like cattle, nay even more astray; those! They are the heedless ones"

[al-A'raaf 7:179]

"Or do you think that most of them hear or understand? They are only like cattle nay, they are even farther astray from the Path (i.e. even worse than cattle)"[al-Furqaan 25:44]

10 – He will be punished eternally

The kaafir will move from one torment to another, in the sense that he will depart from this world – where he is exposed to shocks and calamities – to the Hereafter. In the first stage (of this transition) the angels of death will descend upon him, preceded by the angels of torment who will give him a taste of the punishment that he deserves. Allaah says:

"And if you could see when the angels take away the souls of those who disbelieve (at death); they smite their faces and their backs…"[al-Anfaal 8:50]

Then when his soul has come forth and he is placed in his grave, he is met with a more severe torment. Allaah says, speaking of the people of Pharaoh:

"The Fire, they are exposed to it, morning and afternoon. And on the Day when the Hour will be established (it will be said to the

angels): 'Cause Fir'awn's (Pharaoh) people to enter the severest torment!'"[Ghaafir 40:46]

Then the Day of Resurrection will come and all creatures will be resurrected and shown their deeds, and the kaafir will see that Allaah has listed all of his deeds in that book of which Allaah says (interpretation of the meaning):

"And the Book (one's Record) will be placed (in the right hand for a believer in the Oneness of Allaah, and in the left hand for a disbeliever in the Oneness of Allaah), and you will see the Mujrimoon (criminals, polytheists, sinners), fearful of that which is (recorded) therein. They will say: 'Woe to us! What sort of Book is this that leaves neither a small thing nor a big thing, but has recorded it with numbers!'"[al-Kahf 18:49]

Then the kaafir will wish that he were dust:

"the Day when man will see that (the deeds) which his hands have sent forth, and the disbeliever will say: 'Woe to me! Would that I were dust!'"

[al-Naba' 78:40 – interpretation of the meaning]

Because of the horrors of that situation [on the Day of Resurrection], if a man possessed all that is on earth he would give it to ransom himself from the torment of that Day. Allaah says (interpretation of the meaning):

"And those who did wrong (the polytheists and disbelievers in the Oneness of Allaah), if they had all that is in earth and therewith as much again, they verily, would offer it to ransom themselves therewith" [al-Zumar 39:47]

"The Mujrim, (criminal, sinner, disbeliever) would desire to ransom himself from the punishment of that Day by his children. And his wife and his brother, And his kindred who sheltered him, And all that are in the earth, so that it might save him"

[al-Ma'aarij 70:11-14]

That abode is the abode of requital and not the abode of hope, so man must inevitably face the requital for his deeds: if they were good, then it will be good, and if they were bad, then it will be bad. The worst that the kaafir will encounter on the Day of Resurrection will be the torment of the Fire. Allaah has created different kinds of torment for its inhabitants so that they may taste the consequences of their deeds. Allaah says (interpretation of the meaning):

"This is the Hell which the Mujrimoon (polytheists, criminals, sinners) denied. They will go between it (Hell) and the fierce boiling water!"
[al-Rahmaan 55:43-44]

And He says, describing their drink and clothing (interpretation of the meaning):

"then as for those who disbelieved, garments of fire will be cut out for them, boiling water will be poured down over their heads. With it will melt (or vanish away) what is within their bellies, as well as (their) skins. And for them are hooked rods of iron (to punish them)" [al-Hajj 22:19-21]

https://www.dar-alifta.org/Foreign/ViewFatwa.aspx?ID=5918

Question

I had a conversation with one of my Muslim friends who thinks that Jews and Christians are not disbelievers as disbelief only occurs to the one who denies the existence of God. My opinion is that denying God is not the only reason of disbelief. Would you clarify this please?

Answer

Disbelief has more than one meaning. There is a kind of disbelief which is atheism and this is what your friends meant by this kind of disbelief which indicates the non existence of God. Another meaning of disbelief is disbelieving in Prophet Muhammad (peace be upon him) and this meaning is the one that is meant by Muslims when they call someone as a disbeliever. This understanding of disbelief versus Islam does not necessitate atheism or disbelieving in God because Islam is an open system which does not differentiate between prophets. Therefore Muslims reached a consensus that whoever disbelieves in any of God's prophet while his message is well conveyed to him is a disbeliever even if he admitted the existence of God and believed in all the rest of God's prophets. Therefore, whoever disbelieves in Prophet Moses is a disbeliever and same goes for whoever disbelieves in Prophet Muahmmad after the Prophet's message was well conveyed to him.

https://islamqa.info/en/answers/6688/whoever-does-not-believe-that-the-kaafirs-are-kaafirs-is-himself-a-kaafir

Question

Is it true that anyone who does not accept that kuffaar are kuffaar is a kaafir himself, even if he prays, believes in the

Qur'aan, and the Prophet Muhammad ( )? If so, what is the proof for this? Can a person insist on believing that Jews and Christians can be believers and go to heaven after being shown clear evidence against this, and still be considered a Muslim?

Answer

Praise be to Allah.

Yes, this is correct. Whoever is not convinced that the person who disbelieves in the religion of Allaah is a kaafir, does not believe what Allaah has told us about their being kaafirs, and he does not believe that the religion of Islam abrogates all previous religions and that all people must follow this religion no matter what their religion was before.

Allaah says (interpretation of the meaning):

And whoever seeks a religion other than Islam, it will never be accepted of him, and in the Hereafter he will be one of the losers [Aal Imraan 3:85]

Say (O Muhammad): O mankind! Verily, I am sent to you all as the Messenger of Allaah [al-Araaf 7:158]

Al-Qaadi Ayyaad said: hence we regard as a kaafir everyone who follows a religion other than the religion of the Muslims, or who agrees with them, or who has doubts, or who says that their way is correct, even if he appears to be a Muslim and believes in Islam and that every other way is false, he is a kaafir

(Al-Shifaa bi Tareef Huqooq al-Mustafaa, 2/1071)

Shaykh Muhammad ibn Abd al-Wahhaab (may Allaah have mercy on him) said:

Know that among the greatest things that can nullify Islam are ten things:

1. Associating othes in worship of Allaah alone, Who has no partner or associate. The evidence ofr that is the aayah (interpretation of the meaning):

Verily, Allaah forgives not (the sin of) setting up partners (in worship) with Him, but He forgives whom He wills, sins other than that [al-Nisaa 4:116].

This also includes offering scarifices to other than Allaah, such as to the jinn or at graves.

Whoever regards others as intermediaries between him and Allaah and calls upon them to ask them to intercede for him, is a kaafir according to scholarly consensus.

Whoever does not regard the Mushrikeen as kaafirs or doubts that they are kaafirs or regard their way as correct, is a kaafir according to scholarly consensus.

After enumerating them, he said:

In the case of all these things that nullify Islam, there is no difference whether a person is joking or is serious or is afraid except in cases where he is forced to do something. All of them are among the things that are very dangerous and which happen very often. The Muslim has to beware of them and fear them happening to him. We seek refuge with Allaah from the things that earn His wrath and His painful prunishment, May Allaah bless Muhammad.

(Muallafaat al-Shaykh Muhammad ibn Abd al-Wahhaab, 212, 213).

1. Shirk and kufr are the same when it comes to the ruling (hukm)

Ibn Hazm said:

Kufra and shirk are the same; every kaafir is a mushrik and every mushrik is a kaafir. This is the view of al-Shaafa and others. (al-Fisl, 3/124).

The Jews and Christians are kuffaar and mushrikeen. Allaah says (interpretation of the meaning):

And the Jews say: Uzair (Ezra) is the son of Allaah, and the Christians say: Messiah is the son of Allaah. That is their saying with their mouths, resembling the saying of those who disbelieved aforetime. Allaahs Curse be on them, how they are deluded away from the truth! They (Jews and Christians) took their rabbis and their monks to be their lords besides Allaah (by obeying them in things which they made lawful or unlawful according to their own desires without being ordered by Allaah), and (they also took as their Lord) Messiah, son of Maryam (Mary), while they (Jews and Christians) were commanded [in the Tauraat (Torah) and the Injeel (Gospel)] to worship none but One Ilaah (God Allaah) Laa ilaaha illa Huwa (none has the right to be worshipped but He). Praise and glory be to Him (far above is He) from having the partners they associate (with Him). [al-Tawbah 9:30-31].

It was reported from Abu Hurayrag that the Messenger of Allaah (peace and blessings of Allaah be upon him) said: *By the One is Whose hand is the soul of Muhammad, not one of this nation, Jew or Christian, will hear of me and will die without having believed in that with which I have been sent, but he will be one of the dwellers of Hell fire.*

(Narrated by Muslim, 153)

Whoever says that the Jews are not kaafirs is disbelieving in the words of Allaah (interpretation of the meanings):

And their hearts absorbed (the worship of) the calf because of their disbelief [al-Baqarah 2:93]

Among those who are Jews, there are some who displace words from (their) right places and say: We hear your word (O Muhammad) and disobey, and Hear and let you (O Muhammad) hear nothing. And Raaina [in Arabic it means Be careful, listen to us, and we listen to you, whereas in Hebrew, it means an insult] with a twist of their tongues and as a mockery of the religion (Islâm). And if only they had said: We hear and obey, and Do make us understand, it would have been better for them, and more proper; but Allaah has cursed them for their disbelief

[al-Nisa 4:46]

Because of their breaking the covenant, and of their rejecting the Ayaat (proofs, evidences, verses, lessons, signs, revelations, etc.) of Allaah, and of their killing the Prophets unjustly, and of their saying: Our hearts are wrapped (with coverings, i.e. we do not understand what the Messengers say) nay, Allaah has set a seal upon their hearts because of their disbelief, so they believe not but a little. And because of their (Jews) disbelief and uttering against Maryam (Mary) a grave false charge (that she has committed

[143]

illegal sexual intercourse); And because of their saying (in boast), We killed Messiah Eesaa (Jesus), son of Maryam (Mary), the Messenger of Allaah, but they killed him not, nor crucified him, but it appeared so to them the resemblance of Eesaa (Jesus) was put over another man (and they killed that man)] [al-Nisa 4:155-157]

Verily, those who disbelieve in Allaah and His Messengers and wish to make distinction between Allaah and His Messengers (by believing in Allaah and disbelieving in His Messengers) saying, We believe in some but reject others, and wish to adopt a way in between. They are in truth disbelievers. And We have prepared for the disbelievers a humiliating torment [al-Nisa 4:150-151]

Whoever says that the Christians are not kuffaar is disbelieving in the words of Allaah (interpretation of the meanings): Surely, in disbelief are they who say that Allaah is the Messiah, son of Maryam (Mary) [al-Maaidah 5:17]

Surely, disbelievers are those who said: Allaah is the third of the three (in a Trinity). But there is no Ilaah (god) (none who has the right to be worshipped) but One Ilaah (God Allâh). And if they cease not from what they say, verily, a painful torment will befall on the disbelievers among them [al-Maaidah 5:73]

And he is disbelieving in the words of Allaah concerning the Jews and Christians who do not believe in our Prophet or follow him: *Verily, those who disbelieve in Allaah and His Messengers and wish to make distinction between Allaah and His Messengers (by believing in Allaah and disbelieving in His Messengers) saying, We believe in some but reject others, and wish to adopt a way in between. They are in truth disbelievers. And We have prepared for the disbelievers a humiliating torment*

[al-Nisa 4:150-151]

What is there left to say after these clear statements from Allaah, may He be exalted? We ask Allaah to guide us. May Allaah bless our Prophet Muhammad.

https://www.thesunniway.com/articles/item/263-calling-a-kafir-a-kafir

Question

Respected Mufti Sahib, Someone that says that we mustn't call a kaafir as a kaafir as because what if he died whilst reciting the Shahadah. As we know on the same token a Muslim may be a Muslim but we don't know how he will die. Please enlighten us with the proper Islamic ruling

Answer

Only an ignorant person can make such a comment. All throughout the history of Islam, the magnificent scholars have unanimously agreed that it is a part of Imaan (faith) to know a kafir as a kafir and a Muslim as a Muslim. This is the reason why in their books they have a section named Baab Al-Murtad. All the books of Aqaa'id (Beliefs) and Fiqh (Jurisprudence) have included this section and clearly clarified that whoever did such and such or said such and such is a 'kafir'.

In Bahare Shariat, it says:

"To regard a Muslim a Muslim and a kafir a kafir is from the necessities of faith."

Sadr Al-Shariah further writes:

"Although we cannot say with certainty regarding a specific individual that he died as a Muslim or (may Allah protect) as a kafir until the state of his death is proven by Shar'i evidence; however, this does not mean that one may doubt the kufr of someone who has clearly committed kufr, because doubting the kufr of a clear kafir makes the person a kafir." He further writes: "Judgement in the hereafter will be based on the state at the time of death, but the hukm (rule) of Shariah is based on the apparent. For example, if a kafir such as a Jew, Christian or idol worshipper died, it cannot be said with certainty that he died as a kafir; but it is the command of Allah and His Messenger (peace and blessings be upon him) for us to regard him as a kafir. We must deal with all his matters in his life and after his death as we deal with the matters of every kafir such as: the matters of association; marriage; Salah Al-Janazah; shroud (kafan for the deceased); and burial. When he has committed kufr, then it is an obligation that we know him as a kafir and leave his state of death to Allah (whether he died a kafir or a believer); in the same way as a person who is an apparent Muslim and has not made any statement or committed any action against Imaan (faith), it is an obligation that we must know him as a Muslim, even though we do not know the state he died in."

The tremendous Scholar Qadi Iyad in his Shifaa' writes:

"There is a unanimous consensus upon the kufr of he who does not regard the Jews, Christians or anyone who separates from the religion of the Muslims as a kafir; or he who hesitates in calling them kafir; or he who doubts in this matter. Qadi Abu Bakr (Al-Baaqalani) said: This is because the tawqeef (Shar'i evidence from the Quran and Sunnah upon which none can speak with their own opinion like the number of units in Salah) and the consensus (of the Ummah) both agree upon their kufr; therefore, whoever hesitates or has a doubt in calling them kafir, has rejected the evidence and the tawqeef. Only a kafir would reject or doubt in such a matter."

From the above, one can understand how ignorant a person must be to feel so confident that he is prepared to dispute and differ from not only all the giant scholars all throughout the Islamic history, but also against the unanimous agreement of the Ummah. Yet, he does not wish to stop there; he takes this dispute against Allah and the Messenger of Allah (peace and blessings be upon him) that he will not call a kafir a kafir.

Qadi Iyad further writes in his Shifaa':

"He is a kafir who does not regard those who believe in other than Islam as kafir; or he who hesitates or has doubt in this matter; or he deems their religion correct, even if he himself claims to be a Muslim and apparently deems the rest of the false religions incorrect; he is a kafir for making apparent what he made apparent against that."

Is it not clear that black is black, white is white, water is water, fire is fire, a book is a book, a pen is a pen, a man is a man, a woman is a woman, a child is a child, a Jew is a Jew, a Christian is a Christian, a Buddhist is a Buddhist and a Muslim is a Muslim? Of course it is! Then why is a kafir not a kafir?

If you look in the Quran and Sunnah, you will find that Allah and His beloved Messenger (peace and blessings be upon him) rendered many nominal Muslims kafir. These were people who swore that they were Muslims, performed Salah behind the Prophet Muhammed (peace and blessings be upon him) and even took part in Jihad side by side with the Sahaabah (Allah is pleased with them); but because they uttered a sentence of kufr, Allah and His Messenger (peace and blessings be upon him) rendered them kafir. It is mentioned in Musannaf Ibn Abi Shaybah, Ibn Munzir, the Tafseer of Sheikh Addi Bin Abi Haatim and recorded in Al-Durr Al-Manthoor, by Imam Jalal Al-Deen Al-Suyooti, regarding a man who lost his female camel and came to ask the Messenger of Allah (peace and blessings be upon him) for help. The Messenger of Allah (peace and blessings be upon him) advised him to go to such and such a place and that he would find his camel there. Upon this some people said:

"Muhammad says that such and such a person's camel is in such and such a place; what does he know of the gayb (unseen)?"

These were people who had declared that there is none worthy of worship but Allah Muhammad is the Messenger of Allah; they performed Salah behind the Prophet (peace and blessings be upon him); and they fought in the battlefields under the banner of Allah. When the Prophet (peace and blessings be upon him) was informed of their statement, he called for them and enquired why they said such. They replied: "We were only joking and playing."

Allah, the Almighty and Wise, revealed a verse of the Quran upon this; this is the sixty fifth verse of Surah Al-Tawbah:

"Say O Beloved: Are you joking with Allah, His verses and His Messenger? Do not make excuses, you have become kafir after your Imaan (faith)."

There are several other verses in which Allah has declared some who accepted Islam and became Muslims as kafir, due to an act or a statement. Even in the Hadith, the Messenger of Allah (peace and blessings be upon him) foretold us of people who will be nominal Muslims, yet will not be Muslims. This Hadith in Bukhari Shareef is an eye opener, and one should read it again and again. Sayyiduna Ali (Allah is pleased with him) narrated that the Messenger of Allah (peace and blessings be upon him) said:

"A time will come upon the people in which nothing from Islam will remain but its name; nothing from the Quran will remain but its written form; their Masaajid will be full but empty from guidance; fitnah (corruption) will be released from them and in them, it will return."

In the time of Sayyiduna Ali (Allah is pleased with him), he regarded the khawaarij as kafir and went to war against them; and then there were those who said Ali is worthy of worship. Thus, Sayyiduna Ali regarded them as kafir and ordered for them to be burnt in fire.

This continued all throughout the history of Islam where the Ulema regarded groups who deviated as either misguided or kafir based upon their actions, statements and beliefs. The Messenger of Allah said:

[149]

"When fitnah or innovation becomes apparent and the Scholar does not express his knowledge, then the curse of Allah and the Angels and all the people is upon him."

If we were to follow the ideology of this person, where we do not call a kafir a kafir, because we do not know what is in his heart or in what state he will die, then this would mean that we must not call a Muslim a Muslim, because we do not know what is in his heart or in what state he will die. This would also mean that he cannot call his own father a Muslim or even the Sahabah (Allah is pleased with them) cannot be called Muslims and the pious predecessors, like Imam Abu Hanifah and Imam Shafa'i and Sheikh Abd Al-Qadir Al-Jeelaani, cannot be regarded a Muslim anymore. In the same way, Khumeni cannot be called a kafir, nor can we call Salman Rushdie or George Bush a kafir.

May Allah protect us from such ignorance and keep us firm on the path of the pious predecessors.

Allah knows best and He is most Wise.